COMPUTER CRISIS 2000

W. Michael Fletcher, C.G.A.

Self-Counsel Press
(a division of)
International Self-Counsel Press Ltd.
Canada U.S.A.

*Copyright © 1998 by International Self-Counsel Press Ltd.
All rights reserved.*

No part of this book may be reproduced or transmitted in any form by any means — graphic, electronic, or mechanical — without permission in writing from the publisher, except by a reviewer who may quote brief passages in a review.

Printed in Canada

First edition: January 1998

Canadian Cataloguing in Publication Data

Fletcher, W. Michael, 1950–
   Computer crisis 2000

(Self-counsel series)
ISBN 1-55180-138-8

   1. Year 2000 date conversion (Computer systems) I. Title II. Series.
QA76.76.S64F53 1998   005.1'6   C97-911104-8

Self-Counsel Press
(a division of)
International Self-Counsel Press Ltd.

1481 Charlotte Road   1704 N. State Street
North Vancouver, BC V7J 1H1   Bellingham, WA 98225
Canada   U.S.A.

CONTENTS

PREFACE ... xv

INTRODUCTION:
How this book can help you ... 1

PART I: THE CRISIS THAT TOUCHES US ALL ... 3

1 CRISIS 2000 ... 5
   a. What is this problem, and how did it all happen? ... 5
      1. Cost of memory ... 8
      2. Programs not expected to last ... 9
      3. It matched the human intuitive process ... 9
      4. No linked systems ... 9
      5. Not a new problem ... 10
   b. The thigh bone's connected to the knee bone ... 10
   c. The problem is one of scope ... 12

2 WHO GIVES A FIG ABOUT DATES? ... 13
   a. Possible errors ... 14
      1. Errors in calculations ... 14
      2. Errors in sorting ... 15
      3. Errors in presentation ... 16
      4. Absolute dates ... 16

    b. Leap years   17
    c. Date formats   17
    d. Use of dates in different business functions   18
        1. Accounting   18
        2. Assets   19
        3. Inventory   20
        4. Personnel   20
        5. External dates   21

3 EXCUSES, EXCUSES   23
    a. Five reasons why it won't affect me   23
        1. It affects only big computers, big systems, and big organizations   24
        2. They will find a solution in time   25
        3. If I fix my systems, I'm safe   27
        4. I've got lots of time   27
        5. It's my supplier's problem   28
    b. Three reasons why I don't want to tell my boss   29
        1. No compelling business rationale   30
        2. Not a career-enhancing project   31
        3. Lost opportunities   31
    c. Tactics for delivering the message   32

4 PEOPLE PROBLEMS — PEOPLE POWER   34
    a. Possible on-the-job impact   35
    b. Communication is the key   35
    c. Company directors   36
        1. Responsibilities and liabilities   36
        2. Defensive measures   37

5 TEAM EFFORT: KEEPING ALL
   DEPARTMENTS ON TRACK   46
   a. Information technology (IT)   47
      1. Inventory   47
      2. Backup   49
      3. Software suppliers   50
      4. Mergers and acquisitions   50
      5. Replacement costs and processes   50
   b. Accounting   51
      1. Accounting systems   51
      2. Financial history   52
      3. Audit   52
      4. Budgets   54
      5. Reporting the costs   55
      6. The banker's point of view   57
   c. Other departments   58
      1. Manufacturing and production   58
      2. Purchasing   59
      3. Sales and marketing   59
      4. Personnel and human resources   60
      5. Office operations   61
      6. Retail   61
      7. Facilities management   62
   d. Summary   64

6 IT'S A LEGAL MATTER   65
   a. Directors' and officers' liability   65
   b. Mergers and acquisitions   66
   c. Copyright   66
   d. Class action suits   67

e.	Disclosure obligations	68
f.	Contract liabilities	68
g.	Tax considerations	69
	1. Domestic tax law	70
	2. International tax aspects	70

PART II: THE BIG PICTURE — GOVERNMENT, INFRASTRUCTURE, AND THE BANKS 71

7 WHAT'S BIG BROTHER UP TO? 73

a.	The role of the federal government	73
	1. Internal government systems	73
	2. Taxation	75
	3. Customs and transportation	76
	4. Social security and welfare	79
b.	State and provincial governments	79
	1. Transportation	80
	2. The court system	82
	3. Employment standards	82
c.	Municipal governments	83
	1. Traffic control	83
	2. Water and waste management	84
	3. Fire, police, and ambulance	84
	4. Financing the costs	86
d.	Government readiness	86

8 THE TIES THAT BIND: LOOKING AT
   THE INFRASTRUCTURE   88
   a. Power utilities   89
   b. Water   91
   c. Telecommunications   91
      1. The all-pervasive grid   92
      2. The Internet   92
      3. The telephone PBX system   93
   d. Transportation systems   94
      1. Fuel   94
      2. Schedules   95
   e. What can I do?   96

9 DOLLARS AND SENSE: FINANCIAL
   ORGANIZATIONS AND THE YEAR 2000   98
   a. Banks   99
      1. Failure of deposit and withdrawal systems 100
      2. Failure of reporting systems   100
      3. Failure of service systems   101
      4. Cash withdrawals   102
      5. Bank failures   103
      6. The state of readiness   103
   b. Insurance companies   104
      1. Business interruption insurance   105
      2. Directors' liability insurance   106
      3. Historical data   106
   c. Stock markets and brokerage houses   107
      1. Raising capital   107
      2. Stock market performance   108
      3. Opportunities   110

vii

PART III: YOUR YEAR 2000 PLAN — 113

10 GROUND RULES FOR THE YEAR 2000 PLAN — 115
   a. Rule #1: Ensure top-down support — 116
   b. Rule #2: Form your management committee — 117
   c. Rule #3: Appoint a project leader — 117
   d. Rule #4: Understand the special nature of the project — 118
      1. Scope of the plan — 118
      2. Lack of choice — 119
      3. Time frames — 120
      4. Cost influences — 121
      5. Shortage of resources — 123
   e. Rule #5: Set the schedule — 124
      1. Set your deadlines — 125
      2. Determine how much time you have — 126
      3. Run parallel systems and test — 127
      4. Set those deadlines — again! — 127
   f. Rule #6: Start now! — 128

11 HOW TO HIRE THE RIGHT PERSON FOR THE JOB — 129
   a. Using inside staff — 129
   b. Hiring outside consultants — 132
      1. Determining the tasks — 132
      2. Finding candidates — 133
      3. Setting the criteria — 134
      4. Signing a contract — 134
   c. Caution! Caution! Caution! — 138

12	**TAKING STOCK**	140
	a. Computer hardware	141
	b. Software	142
	c. Systems	143
	d. Other equipment and machinery	145
	e. Customers and suppliers	146
	f. Inventory alert! Considerations for specialized products	147
	1. Specialized software issues	147
	2. Specialized systems issues	149
	g. Summary	150
13	**THE THREE Rs: REPAIR, REPLACE, RETIRE**	152
	a. How to make the choice	153
	1. Hardware	153
	2. Software	153
	3. Systems	154
	b. Repair	155
	1. Advantages	155
	2. Disadvantages	155
	3. Alternative repair	156
	c. Replace	157
	1. Advantages	158
	2. Disadvantages	159
	d. Retire	159
	1. Advantages	159
	2. Disadvantages	159
	e. Outsourcing	160
	1. Advantages	160
	2. Disadvantages	160

14	**GETTING YOUR INVENTORY IN SHAPE**		161
	a. Hardware		162
	1. Computer chips		162
	2. Fixing the chips		163
	b. Software		164
	c. Other hardware components		165
	d. Non-computer equipment		166
	e. Get it in writing — every time!		167
15	**TRIAGE: ESTABLISHING PRIORITIES FOR YOUR SYSTEMS**		169
	a. What will it mean for my business?		170
	b. Systems: subjective analysis		172
	c. Choosing the criteria		173
16	**YOUR COMMUNICATIONS PLAN**		176
	a. The inside job — communicating the plan to staff		177
	b. Go tell the world: communicating the plan to your suppliers and customers		179
	1. Plan carefully		180
	2. Suppliers		182
	3. Customers		183

PART IV: AND NOW FOR THE GOOD NEWS...   185

17 YEAR 2000 OPPORTUNITIES   187
- a. Operational review   187
  1. ISO certification   189
  2. Disaster recovery planning   189
- b. Strategic planning   191
- c. Year 2000 certification   193
  1. Proving your own compliance   193
  2. Proving your customers' and suppliers' compliance   194
  3. International standards   194
- d. Taking advantage of market changes   196
- e. The year 2000 investor   198

PART V: AS THE WORLD TURNS   201

18 THE INTERNATIONAL SCENE   203
- a. Why is so little happening?   203
  1. Difference in calendars   205
  2. Concept of time   205
  3. Government processes   205
- b. Around the globe   207
  1. Canada   208
  2. United States   212
  3. Europe   215
  4. Russia and Eastern Europe   216
  5. Asia   217
  6. South Pacific   218

19	CONCLUSION	219
	a. Owners, managers, and senior executives	220
	b. Employees	220
	c. Professionals and consultants	221
	d. Association members	221
	e. Consumers	222
	f. Voters	222
	g. More support from us	223

APPENDIXES

1	A checklist for chief executive officers of small- and medium-sized enterprises	225
2	Resources	229

TABLES

#1	Year 2000 impact on jobs	41
#2	Percentage of time of whole project spent on individual segments	121
#3	Questions to ask prospective consultants	135

To my wife, Valerie, who still has a hard time believing that such a small computer glitch can cause such havoc.

To my daughters, Caroline, Paula, and Blythe, even though they have reached the stage of considering me monomaniacal about the subject.

To Tracy Trottier-White, who is helping me develop a series of products and seminars to help businesses and who insists that I stay focused on one item long enough to finish it.

To my parents, who taught me that helping other people to grow provides the biggest satisfaction of all.

PREFACE

I am a relative latecomer to the year 2000 problem. When I first started reading about it in 1996, I initially fell into the trap of believing that this was a problem for big systems in big organizations. But I soon came to realize that it had a huge impact on almost everyone on the planet. By early 1997, I started to research the subject from the point of view of small- and medium-sized enterprises, bringing my broad general background to bear on the sorts of issues that these organizations would face as they realized the impact on their operations. At the same time, I was waiting for the media coverage that would awaken people to the issue and for them to start calling on consultants like me to come and help them with the inventory, project planning, and management challenges they would face. Here I am in late 1997 still waiting for that worldwide alarm.

Where is the press coverage of how important this glitch could be to all businesses if they do not start protecting themselves? Where are the government action plans for planning and prevention measures? Where are the business and association newsletters to their members about the problem, their urgent reminders of how little time is left, their demands of the various levels of government to do more and to do it faster? Where are the surveys showing that the great majority of companies are aware of the problem and are well into their contingency planning?

In a word, missing.

Banks and insurance companies started running into miscalculations in their mortgage and investment programs in the early 1980s. In the late 1980s government departments discovered they had problems. Particular industries, such as magazine publishing, started encountering invalid subscription expires in 1995 and 1996. It is only because the mainstream media have recently caught up with the topic that this issue has suddenly surfaced.

But generally, time and time again, as I talked to businesspeople, I heard that the issue didn't apply to them. They told me that it affected big companies, but not their smaller ones. It affected mainframe computers, but not their PCs (personal computers). They told me that their programs were off the shelf from reputable companies, and that the year 2000 problem was an issue only for those companies with millions of lines of COBOL (a programming language) code, not them. I realized that they didn't understand, and that no one was telling them the truth.

And so I wrote this book. As I sit here doing the final edit, I have to hold back my impulse to explain more fully, to give more examples, to do more research. That might make it a more comprehensive resource, but it would delay the process of getting it into your hands, and speed is of the essence. I hope the value of the information contained in it outweighs any errors or omissions you may find, for which I take sole responsibility. The book is primarily designed to be a guide for small- and medium-sized businesses. I have written it in the hope that it will help everyone understand the problem, whether producer or consumer, employee or executive. But I especially want to reach the small- and medium-sized business entrepreneur. I hope you find it helps.

INTRODUCTION
How this book can help you

The first part of this book (chapters 1 to 6) outlines the background of the problem, both within individual enterprises and through their "dependencies," those interconnected interests that will affect them. The second part of the book (chapters 7 to 9) discusses dependencies and infrastructures. Part III (chapters 10 to 16) outlines your year 2000 plan. Part IV (chapter 17) highlights some opportunities available to businesses from the year 2000 crisis — it's not all bad news! Part V (chapters 18 and 19) describes the international scene.

As I was writing this book, I found that there were many areas where I could devote an entire chapter to a single subject or institution. I resisted the temptation to do so. I certainly want to convince you that the problem is real and must be addressed as fast as possible by all enterprises, but this book is not designed to be an exhaustive treatise on the causes and effects of the year 2000 crisis. There is a lot more information available on any specific year 2000 topic, and I encourage you to become as completely informed as possible on all aspects of the situation. (Appendix 2 provides you with an excellent list of sources to help start you on that research.)

As I've noted earlier, I wrote this book primarily for small- and medium-sized enterprises. I am convinced that the vast majority of you have not had the information about this issue presented in such a way to show you that it is an issue for *your* business. You will find my information and explanations useful, but more important, I hope that you take action on them. Use the information in this book to help your own business, or bring it to the attention of your company's senior management to develop plans on a corporate-wide basis. Start a local or industry committee to raise awareness, or spend some effort insisting that governments at all levels take this issue seriously. The biggest risk we face is that of inaction.

Although I wrote the book for a North American audience, its comments are applicable to businesses the world over. North America is probably most at risk because of the high level of computerization in business and government, but I believe that there are many countries in the world that may also be at major risk from the year 2000 problem. Small businesses overseas that use manual systems and operate in local markets, may continue to operate as usual. This is not the case in Canada and the United States. If this were a crisis that would affect government alone, we might have the resources to deal with it. However, our industries are intimately tied to computers, and our computers are far more interconnected than those elsewhere. This may make the year 2000 issue far more serious for enterprises in the industrialized world.

> If you assume that only 10% of the programming code in the world needs correction (and it is a lot more), that means 30 billion lines of code need correction. If there are 100 million businesses worldwide and 98% of them survive this crisis, that means two million businesses will fail.

This is an unprecedented challenge on a global basis. The best way we as individuals can deal with it is to take care of it step by step for our own enterprises. In doing so, we may solve it in the best possible way for the portion of the world over which we ourselves have maximum influence.

PART I

THE CRISIS THAT TOUCHES ALL OF US

1
CRISIS 2000

a. WHAT IS THIS PROBLEM, AND HOW DID IT ALL HAPPEN?

The year 2000 problem is going to affect everyone.

EVERYONE.

- Whether you deal with mainframe computers or PCs, it will affect you.
- Whether you have a computer in your business or not, it will affect you.
- Whether you are in the public or private sector, it will affect you.
- Whether you are in the retail, service, manufacturing, or finance sector, it will affect you.
- Whether you are in sales, accounting, production, or management, it will affect you.

- Whether you work in an office, have your business in your home, or are a homemaker, it will affect you.

If you take away only one thing from reading this book, please let it be this: far too many people believe either that the issue does not affect them or that it touches them in so peripheral a way that they have nothing to worry about. In this particular instance, ignorance is not bliss, and it may in fact be an invitation to disaster.

If you are already aware of the year 2000 problem and what it means to computer programs, you may wish to skip this section and move ahead to section **b.** below. Please read that section carefully, because it will alert you to the extent of the problem in our society and how it will affect your business and day-to-day life.

The year 2000 problem — also known as "Y2K" or the "Millennium Bug" — arises from the assumption that because we know which century we are in, all of the equipment around us also understands which century it is. As individuals, we make this assumption all the time. I was born in '50 and grew up in the '60s. I finished studying at York University in '72, and completed my CGA (Certified General Accountant) program in '82 and....well, you get the point. In all the decades and years mentioned, you automatically placed a century date of "19" in front of the other figures. My birth year becomes 1950, my CGA graduation 1982, and so on.

When computer programmers first set up computer instructions in the 1960s and 1970s, they followed the same convention. Certainly it was more formalized, and since computers are essentially logic devices, a program's logic had to be very rigorous. There were other constraints that made using this convention attractive, but it made intuitive as well as logical sense to set it up this way.

As human beings, when we enter the next century we will automatically make the necessary mental adjustments: if someone speaks of '96, we will assume he or she means 1996. If someone mentions '02, we will assume he or she means 2002.

Many computers, though, will not make that intuitive leap. Computers are logic devices, though we may think of them as machines that think. The logic that has been built into most computers is that any date inserted into them is in the 20th century, which means the year starts with the two digits "19."

Herein lies the problem: as we draw closer to the 21st century, we will start to use year dates for the next century, both when we speak and when we enter them into computer programs. However, many computers will not understand that we have moved into a new millennium. When we say "02," meaning 2002, the computer logic and all of its subsequent calculations will assume that we are referring to the year 1902.

The year 2000 problem stems from a decision made in the early days of computer hardware and software design to save storage and memory space by using the two last digits only in a year date in any data field in a computer program. This was initially a software programming problem, but it found its way into the hardware configuration of large computers and eventually into the components of personal computers as well. It's also been programmed into computer chips found in all kinds of appliances and devices, many of which use dates as part of their internal programs to tell them when to take certain actions.

Less than a thousand days from the time I write this, the calendar will turn to January 1, 2000. An enormous number of computers and other devices will not be able to recognize dates in the new century, or they will make miscalculations about what is meant. And when that happens, problems and errors will start occurring that will affect every one of us in our businesses and personal lives.

> http://java.state.ak.us/HyperNews/get/te
> chtalk/7/3.html
>
> Date: Tue, 27 May 1997 19:09:30 GMT
>
> From: XArsenal@juno.com
>
> We have got a big problem. Every computer system older than about 2 years is going to die. The phone companies, power companies — EVERYTHING. It is all because of those idiots who wrote the COBOL language. They were too lazy to write 01/01/1999, so they just made it 01/01/99. So in 2000 it will be like time just stopped. The Hawaiian Electric Company in Japan ran a test with the Y2K bug and they said when the clock hit 2000 the plant just shut down.

With the advantage of hindsight, it is easy to criticize the original programmers who made the decision to include only two digits for the year. As the above Web posting shows, some people respond with very simplistic answers when they are asked how this situation arose. However, 30 years ago there were many strong justifications to support their position.

1. Cost of memory

The most important justification for limiting dates to two digits was the extremely high cost of computer memory. When the first credit card systems were installed in major North American department stores in the late 1960s and early 1970s, the main core of their RAM (random-access memory) consisted of perhaps 64 kilobytes. Today, this amount of RAM would be completely inadequate to run even the simplest of microcomputer programs. Yet in 1970, this was adequate to deal with the transactions of millions of accounts.

I recently bought a new computer and its configuration included 32 megabytes of RAM. This represents 32 million bytes or characters, and it cost less than $400. Thirty years ago, the cost of 32,000 characters — one-tenth of 1% of the 1997 memory — would have cost over $1 million!

2. Programs not expected to last

Another justification for the two-digit year programming decision was that few programmers expected their code to be in use for more than 30 years. Since then new programming languages have been developed that use memory far more effectively than the COBOL and FORTRAN of the early computer years. However, at the same time that the cost of memory has dropped dramatically, computing power has increased enormously. Therefore, though the old codes may be inefficient, large systems continue to use it. It's still more competitive to go with the old code rather than incur the huge costs of rewriting it entirely.

3. It matched the human intuitive process

As human beings, we like to abbreviate things; it saves us time and effort. Therefore, it seemed reasonable to reduce the year code to the last two digits. We're used to seeing dates entered this way and it reduces the time we spend on regularly performed tasks, such as setting standing alarms on our clock radio or speed dials on our telephone system. We even call the year 2000 problem "Y2K."

This casual human approach works just as well on a computer system, provided the logic is rigidly applied. But, as one of my favorite aphorisms states, "The problem with common sense is that it is not very common." That's the problem with an intuitive leap like a change in century; by its very nature, it cannot be programmed into a logical process.

4. No linked systems

It's easy to forget how things used to be. In a world of local area networks (LANs), electronic data interchanges (EDIs), modems, and other communication devices, it is easy to forget that only three decades ago computers worked on a standalone basis. Even within a company, they were divorced from other company operations and sat in their own specially constructed rooms with technicians who wore special clothing. The notion that information from one computer would flow to another, let alone to many others, was inconceivable.

So systems were designed to be self-sufficient. When the occasion arose to get them to talk to each other, the programming twists and turns needed to facilitate this were considerable. In other words, programmers didn't try to reexamine or rework the original set of processes; their solution was to add an adaptation to earlier premises.

5. Not a new problem

This problem arose earlier in this century. In some systems in the 1960s, programmers used a single digit to identify the year, and the system was programmed to expect that not only would the century be "19" but also the decade would be "6." For some companies, there was a mini year 2000 problem at the beginning of 1970 when systems with this design failed to perform date calculations correctly.

b. THE THIGH BONE'S CONNECTED TO THE KNEE BONE

As human beings, we are not very good at thinking about large problems or in long time frames. It is very complicated to think about and evaluate large systems that may involve hundreds, thousands, or even millions of components.

Take the car you use, for example. In a simple trip from home to the store, you may believe that it is operating on its own, or at least that its operation depends only on the interaction between the driver and the vehicle. But if you look a little further, there is a whole set of related systems on which the car depends.

For example, you need gas and oil for the car to run. When something breaks, you need spare parts as well as a mechanic to fix it. You need roads on which to run and traffic control systems to stay safe. A bank or a leasing company is probably involved in the purchase and ownership of the vehicle, and an insurance company is providing coverage in the event of any accident.

If you consider the manufacture of the car itself, the systems get even more numerous and interrelated. Hundreds of companies provide thousands of parts for its manufacture. Many, if not all, of these businesses will use computers. If one of the systems for one of the companies fails, and a part, service, or product cannot be delivered at the right place and at the right time, you may not be able to take the car from point A to point B.

All the systems we use day by day are related, directly or indirectly, to computers. It is this message that has not been clearly presented when the issue of the year 2000 problem has been raised. People think that if they do not work directly with large computers or do not deal with systems that contain millions of lines of custom-written code, it will have no effect on their lives. But the reality is that individual systems are all part of an integrated whole, extending from the company level out to a region, an industry, a national economy, and the whole global society.

Understanding this concept is crucial. It is only when you accept that "their" problem could well be your problem that you will start looking at the connections that are critical to your business and start to take the steps to protect your operations and your partners'. It can't be repeated often enough:

(a) The problem extends to all kinds of computers, including personal computers. This means that it affects all kinds of enterprises, not just large ones.

(b) Besides computers, the problem also extends to all kinds of computer chips. Whether we realize it or not, these devices surround us and touch all of our lives.

(c) We are all intimately involved with the problem because computers of all kinds are deeply integrated into all of our social and economic systems.

c. THE PROBLEM IS ONE OF SCOPE

Even when people understand the problem, their first reaction is that it is easy to fix. In a way they are right. It's not the mechanics of fixing a date field that is the challenge, rather it is the sheer number and variety of date fields that need to be considered.

Imagine you have been asked to change a light bulb. No problem. You take the replacement bulb, unscrew the old one, screw in the new one, and flick the switch. What could be simpler?

Now imagine that you have been asked to change every light bulb in your community. That includes small 60-watt bulbs, large 100-watt globes, neon tubes, car headlights, refrigerator lights, traffic signals, desk lamps, flashlights, store signs, and Christmas illuminations. You don't know where they all are and some of the doors to get to them are locked, with no keys. In addition, you know you don't have enough spares, you will have to work in the dark to find some of them, and you must accomplish this entire task in the next two weeks.

THAT is the nature of the year 2000 problem. The challenge is one of location, access, analysis, resources, spares, knowledge, and time. It could have been fixed with no problem if we had started early enough. We didn't and so we have created a monster impossible to conquer in the time remaining.

2
WHO GIVES A FIG ABOUT DATES?

Two millennia ago, no one paid any attention to the time, and everyone operated on the basis of a "general feel" for the time of day combined with a knowledge of the seasons. In fact, farmers still work this way. On a farm, the precise time of day is less important than the seasons, which dictate when crops need to be planted and harvested.

Ever since the first reliable clocks were invented approximately 500 years ago, society in general — and Western society in particular — has been increasingly governed by the time and the date. Our demand for accuracy of time and date is integrated into most of our societal systems, as well as both the foreground and background of our computer systems.

For example, your birth date is one of the pieces of information that gets recorded when you apply for a driver's license. There will be a calculation in the program to figure out how old you are and when it will be time to send out a notice for your license renewal. And there will also be a date that is attached to the computer record itself, telling when that file was created, updated, or last accessed, and perhaps also influencing when it is backed up or deleted.

So even if you think you are able to exist with only an occasional glance at a watch or a calendar, you need to realize that the systems around you are constantly using dates to make calculations and organize events in your life. From the alarm clock that wakes you in the morning, to bus and subway schedules you depend on to get to work on time, everything depends on the date. Think of your company's payroll; it's set up to be paid to employees on a specific day, and payments for their mortgages, cars, loans, and other bills depend on that money being paid at a scheduled time.

Most of our systems rely on dates, either as a point in time or in order to calculate the time between two dates. So you can see how many other systems and schedules will be affected if the date provided to those systems is wrong, or a date cannot be provided at all.

a. POSSIBLE ERRORS

When computer clocks change over to January 1, 2000, a variety of errors may occur — all of them the result of the fact that computers will not understand the date correctly. In most cases, a computer will continue to assume that the century date is 19, i.e., that we are still in the 20th century. If you enter January 1, 00, on the first day of the new millennium, many computers will assume that the year is 1900.

What sort of problems will this cause? Errors in calculations, sorting, presentation, and absolute dates...for starters.

1. Errors in calculations

First, there will be errors in calculation. If you were born in 1965, for example, you will be 34 years old in 1999, the calculation being 1999 - 1965 = 34. But if you enter the year

2000 into the calculation, a computer system would translate the date "00" as 1900. The calculation will then become 1900 - 1965, which gives the result as -65. In many programming languages, the minus sign would be lost, so the result would be 65.

Other errors in calculation may occur just because the information that results from the date calculation is incomplete. For example, let us suppose that it is June 1, 2000. If you ask for a list of customers who have made purchases since January 1, 2000, your system may not give you a single name of anyone who has made a purchase in the last six months. Or, worse still, if you tell your database to erase everyone older than five years old, you could well wind up erasing all of your most recent clients!

2. Errors in sorting

Those of you who work with spreadsheets may have already run across an error when you try to sort a list of numbers. If the computer thinks it is dealing with text, it will sort the numbers with the same logic that a dictionary sorts words; that is, all numbers starting with 1 would come first, then all numbers starting with 2, and so on. This means that 111 would come before 12, and also before 23.

To see an example of this type of sorting, look in the Help Index or the manual of a spreadsheet program, such as Quattro Pro or Excel. There you will see that the listing "1900 date system" comes before "24 hour clock," and "360 day year" comes before "3-D charts."

When it comes to the year 2000, this method of sorting will cause errors because "00" will be sorted before "99." If there is a list of dates stored in a YYMMDD format (in other words, without the century), a date of 00/05/16 (i.e., May 16, 2000) will be sorted as being before 99/10/21 (October 21, 1999). This could affect everything that depends on accurate inventory records — from a company's purchases over the years to maintenance schedules for machinery.

3. Errors in presentation

The century date of 19xx is printed into many documents, or may be "hard-coded" into computer systems. (Take a look at the checks you have for your personal account!) So dates displayed on documents such as invoices may come out as 1900 because the system's program can recognize only the last two digits of the year.

4. Absolute dates

Unfortunately, not even the inconsistency in date calculations will be consistent. A lot of chips and programs will assume that "00" means that the year is 1900. But for various reasons related to the development of the Intel computer chips, some will say that the date is 1980 and some will believe that it is 1984. So it may not even be possible to make a single correction that will be valid for all chips. Worse, it could even be that different computers in your network will reset to different dates because they have different chips inside.

Absolute dates of this type are important; in many cases, these are the dates that a computer system will automatically stamp on files as they are changed. Networks will often back up the latest files and manipulate others, possibly erasing those that are over a certain age. If you are not ready for this, you could find that not only is all of your latest work not being backed up, but it is also being carefully erased each night by a system that assumes the information is so old that it is redundant.

This information is also key for those of you who have a proper series of backups and a set of regular procedures to make copies of key company information and data. Usual procedures for such utilities are to compare the date on the old backup with the current file date. If the new file date is more recent, it will back it up; if not, it will ignore it. But in this case the "old" file may be newer than the "new" one. And replacing all the backup files with those dated in 1980 or 1984 may not work, as there may be a number of old files that you truly don't want to replace with the backups.

b. LEAP YEARS

Most people know the basic rule for leap years: if a year can be divided by four, it is a leap year and there will be a February 29 in it. There are two additional rules to help calculate leap years correctly. The second rule is that if it's a century year, it may be divisible by four, but it will *not* be a leap year. The third rule is that if a century year can be divided by 400, then it *is* a leap year. By following these rules, it becomes clear that the year 2000 is a leap year.

However, there are some computer programs as well as microchips that do not realize the year 2000 is a leap year. Chips that fail to calculate the leap year correctly may start with valid calculations as of January 1, 2000, but will then start to make errors as of March 1 because they fail to recognize that there is a February 29, 2000.

c. DATE FORMATS

Another difficulty in locating the fields that may be affected by the year 2000 problem is that there is not one single format that has been followed in entering date fields into programs. In some cases the day is presented first, in some cases the month, and in some cases the year. So the date format can be any combination of fields, including DDMMYY, MMDDYY, YYDDMM, YYMMDD. And these are the most simple examples, where the date field is not combined with an invoice number or purchase order. In other cases the field itself is encrypted to make sure that unauthorized individuals cannot find out where the date field is, let alone what value is inside it.

Dates are also relative. While one company may need the detail of an exact month or day, others may be more interested in the season, or in the number of production batches entered in the month. So date equations have been invented for all possible variations. Some accounting systems, for example, use 13 periods of four weeks each in order to be able to provide exact comparisons between periods. These periods are unadjusted as to whether the month has 31 or 28 days in it. There are other programs that, while still using six digits in the date field, put the date in as a numerical value, representing the number of days since the start of the century, i.e., the number of days since January 1, 1900.

And finally, just to complicate the situation still further, some programs store these references as a single number, some with dashes or slashes, some with spaces, and....well, you get the picture.

d. USE OF DATES IN DIFFERENT BUSINESS FUNCTIONS

As I said earlier, time and date stamps are now something that we take for granted, and most people will be able to immediately think of times when the date needs to be consciously added, for example, in accounting applications for invoices and checks. The extent to which date calculations are used affects almost every department, even though the use of dates may be going on only in the background.

1. Accounting

The way in which accounting has evolved, particularly in the way it tries to provide meaningful information to management, means that date calculations are a key component in almost all accounting transactions. One of the key generally accepted accounting principles (GAAP) is that of matching

— matching revenue and expense items within a specific period. This is the reason accruals (estimates of amounts related to the calendar period being calculated) are made at the end of each month where, for a variety of reasons, exact information is not available.

Aside from financial statements, however, the date is used in almost every other kind of financial transaction. In many cases, the date occurs in the background, without it specifically being entered by a data entry clerk or computer programmer. For example, an accounting system may deal with automatic payments to suppliers or a bank. It calculates interest payable. It will produce reports on the aging of accounts receivable and accounts payable. It will calculate variances between actual expenditures and budget amounts, matching both to specific date segments of the financial year.

2. Assets

A subset of accounting, and one that is very important in safeguarding the property owned by a business, is that of asset management, which deals with all kinds of machinery, equipment, and other possessions, such as cars and buildings. Apart from maintaining accurate lists of these items together with a dollar amount of their value, accounting systems also calculate depreciation, which is an estimate of the items' allocated cost over their useful life. In addition, the program will keep track of maintenance and repair of these assets and will help calculate when equipment should be retired or replaced.

An increasing number of assets are now rented or leased. Regular monthly, quarterly, or annual payments, based on specific dates, are made in order for the company to retain possession of the assets and to be able to continue to use them. Failure to make these payments means that the equipment is liable to be removed from the company premises. Besides needing an accurate calendar to keep track of such payments and do the necessary calculations, a company will often, at the end of its lease or rental contract, have a number of options, such as the right to renew the lease or to buy the asset for a fixed price. So the dates involved in such agreements are important, allowing a business to make informed decisions concerning the purchase of assets or the return and/or replacement of assets.

3. Inventory

Inventory control is very important to a small business as it relates to manufacturing and production. For many companies, the investment in inventory represents a significant part of their financial assets. This means that money spent on raw materials and parts is money that cannot be invested elsewhere.

Inventory also represents the amount of production that a company can do in the short and medium term. A larger amount of inventory, while representing a larger dollar investment, also means that the company can produce more goods while not having to wait for shipments from suppliers. Dates play a crucial role in establishing the optimum level of inventory, as well as providing a production manager with schedules indicating when replacements must be ordered.

A specialized form of inventory control is called just-in-time (JIT) inventory, where the minimum amount of materials are held on site but require ongoing deliveries to make sure that a company can continue production. This sort of system cannot function without precise calendar management.

4. Personnel

The other area of company operations that uses dates in all aspects of its day-to-day work is human resources. Some of the dates included in an individual's personnel file may include date of hiring, first day on the job, birth date, date of next salary review, date of a cost of living adjustment, benefits eligibility date, date of last physical examination, dates of training taken, and termination date.

Personnel dates are also used on a day-to-day basis for all kinds of schedules, particularly in a production environment. Dates in these cases may be related more to clock times than calendar times, but the principle remains the same. Start and end times for shifts, calculation of overtime breaks, time off, travel allowances, meal charges, and many other items are date-related.

Finally, in an increasingly electronic world, where most workers are linked by computers, dates are also important in human resource uses. E-mail automatically puts a date and time on interoffice communication, and many companies use electronic schedules to set the times for meetings or to book the availability of board rooms and other locations.

5. External dates

As offices and different organizations become increasingly interconnected by computer, we need to rely on the accuracy of dates provided by third parties. Events like license renewals, inspection dates, and insurance renewals are just some of the schedules that must be coordinated with other companies and individuals. On the financial end, on both a business and personal level, there are automatic purchases, loan payments for items like mortgages and cars, as well as other financial transactions to be concerned about.

External dates are also very important to all kinds of travel arrangements. In fact, a travel itinerary is entirely made up of a series of dates. From the date and times of flights, arrangements for car rentals, meeting times, and other business appointments to hotel reservations and wake-up calls, dates are key to the efficient organization of a travel schedule. As we do more international traveling, where changes in time zones complicate an itinerary even further, we rely more and more on accurate clocks.

The more you think about this issue, the more occasions you can establish where dates are a key part of a business. And the fact that computers are linked in so many ways, whether directly or indirectly, means that we rely on accurate information, including date information, to be transferred from one system to another on a minute-by-minute basis.

We are all connected: upstream are our suppliers, downstream are our customers. And like it or not, there are almost no companies that are not an integrated part of some economic chain within our society. This is perhaps the key reason why small- and medium-sized enterprises must become aware of the year 2000 problem and start to address the implications it has for each and every one of our businesses.

3
EXCUSES, EXCUSES

a. FIVE REASONS WHY IT WON'T AFFECT ME

Presumably you have now reluctantly reached the conclusion that this is, indeed, a real problem, and one with no single easy solution. It is now a business issue of major proportions, one that will affect government and home operations as well. Why is no one taking it more seriously?

Even for those aware of the problem, there are a variety of reasons given for why there is no need to spend a lot of time thinking about it. And as you prepare to convince people in your enterprise that they must take this issue seriously, expect excuses — and be ready to counter them. The most frequent ones include:

(a) It affects only big computers, big systems, and big organizations.

(b) They will find a solution in time.

(c) If I fix my systems, I'm safe.

(d) I've got lots of time.

(e) It's my supplier's problem.

A look at each of these excuses shows that they are simplistic and betray an ignorance of the real situation.

1. It affects only big computers, big systems, and big organizations

It is true that the most immediate and significant effect of the year 2000 problem will be on large systems. However, all computer systems, even personal computers for home use, contain one or more date-dependent chip, primarily in a chip called the BIOS (basic input/output system), and another called the RTC (real time clock). The computer uses these for a number of date-related functions that may be hidden from the average microcomputer user but which nevertheless affect the overall ability of the computer to function properly.

Since personal computers are affected, the size of company affected immediately drops from one with hundreds of employees and mainframe computers to any business that has a single PC — which means almost every business in North America.

The other fallacy with this comment is that it fails to recognize the large number of systems that operate in our day-to-day environment. Though not computers, these systems can operate only with the help of computer chips and other electronic systems in which date-related chips have been embedded. Even if every computer system in the world could be easily fixed, the existence of millions of such chips in devices around the globe would present a fundamental problem by themselves.

Note: As of the time of writing in mid-1997, many microcomputers were still being sold with "problem" chips. According to the Information Technology Association of America (ITAA), as many as 47% of the computers being sold today are still not equipped to correctly handle the year 2000 problem. This figure alone doesn't even start to address the millions of computers sold over the last 15 years, many of which are still operating in businesses around the world.

2. They will find a solution in time

Even when businesspeople recognize that the problem extends beyond large systems, it is common to hear the comment that "someone already has the solution and is just waiting to release it." This is also known as the silver bullet solution.

But who is the "they" that people refer to? Most often it is Microsoft, the largest software company in the world. Even Microsoft has not formally announced that all of its current tools are year 2000 compliant, and it would have a significant problem providing "patches" to all the older versions of its software still running around the globe. The people who make this comment fail to recognize the sheer complexity of the problem: its size, the availability of resources, and the cost.

First, let's consider the size. Informed sources estimate that there are between 300 and 600 billion lines of code in operation throughout the world. The majority of these are written in Cobol, C, and Assembler, but there are literally hundreds of languages in day-to-day use. Now add in the millions of programs written to enhance spreadsheets such as Lotus 123 or older databases such as dBase. Now add in the hundreds of operating systems (e.g., DOS, Windows 3.1, Windows 95, dozens of varieties of Unix, OS/2). These are running on hundreds of millions of computers worldwide, and the computers are located in tens of millions of companies. And we haven't even considered the billions of embedded chips.

Second, there are not enough resources. Even with an ever-increasing number of automated tools being developed every day, there are not enough trained personnel able to operate them or to oversee the project management of correcting all the necessary programs. This is the case even if you consider only those organizations that recognize they have a problem today, and the scarcity of resources is already driving prices up. If you add to this the number of companies that will recognize they have a problem in the next year or so, the lack of resources becomes overwhelming.

Even if there were no problem related to the year 2000, there is already a significant shortage of people trained in software technology. In Canada, there is an estimated need for 30,000 to 40,000 individuals in a wide range of interesting and highly paid positions. In the United States, the demand is ten times this amount. Our education system is grappling with the problem of satisfying this demand, without considering how it can provide training in computer languages that in many cases were dead 20 years ago.

Finally, consider the cost. Even if we had the personnel needed to complete the conversion, the dollars to do so are simply not being made available by most governments, nor by the private sector. If the cost of converting a system is $1 per line, the total cost would be somewhere between $300 and $600 billion. Given that the entire world economy amounts to US $27.8 trillion a year, suddenly adding 1% to this amount (or removing it from other activities) represents an enormous adjustment of priorities. This is made even more difficult by the fact that many countries and governments haven't acknowledged that there is a problem in the first place.

So it's not possible for there to be a silver bullet! There can't be one simple solution that will apply to every computer, to every application, to every piece of data, and to every chip. Don't rely on someone else to solve it all, and pretend that you need do nothing.

3. If I fix my systems, I'm safe

Anyone who offers this as an excuse fails to appreciate how dependent we are on other people's computer systems and how interrelated all our computers have become.

The best analogy I have found is to consider the year 2000 problem as a large computer virus that has affected every computer system in the world. On that basis, no company would clean the virus off its own computers and confidently announce that from that point on it had nothing to fear. It would understand that the moment it received any information from another system, the problem would start all over again. That's the crux of the year 2000 issue. Your accounting system's compliance is useless if your bank is unable to provide you with access to the money in your account. An inventory control system's precision is of no value if your suppliers' operations are so inadequate that they cannot provide you with any inventory in the first place.

Furthermore, it will be difficult to identify what system is dependent on what: who on whom. This challenge calls for an entire communication plan of its own, which I discuss in chapter 16. Even if a company tries to ask all of its "dependents" whether or not they are compliant, their lack of understanding means that their responses can't be trusted.

4. I've got lots of time

If you're like most people, you've been guilty at some point in your life of underestimating the amount of time that it takes to do something. As organizations become more complicated, it is also more difficult for any one individual to fully appreciate the ramifications of large-scale system changes. As of January 1, 1998, there will be barely 700 days left to the millennium, which translates into only 100 weeks of work. For many companies, to add this workload to all existing programs — and require 100% accuracy upon completion — represents a major logistical problem.

More important is that many companies won't have 100 working weeks available to them. If a company's 1999 fiscal year end is on August 31, for example, it will need to have a complete conversion done by that date. And if it wants a "comfort zone" to ensure that whatever changes made to its accounting systems are 100% accurate (close is not good enough), it should, in fact, have a full year of clean operation on its system *before* it has to deal with any dates involving the year 2000. This means that its system should be completely converted by August 31, 1998. So from January 1 to August 31, 1998, a business has a scant eight months to do all that is needed, including identifying what it needs, evaluating what products are available, selecting one, organizing the charts of accounts and other necessary data, setting up the system, training the personnel, doing all the conversions, documenting all the procedures, running parallel for a couple of months, and finally completing the changeover. Keep in mind that all this is necessary to convert just *one* of a company's systems.

Once again, this timetable fails to consider the interdependencies of all business systems. Do you repair what you have or do you replace it? Is intercompany testing required? Must your company convert first to allow another sister organization to follow afterward? Should you establish an industry standard, a process which, although valuable, will absorb a huge amount of time? What other ongoing priorities will be curtailed or delayed in order to free up the resources needed? Do you have the capital required for all the necessary purchases?

5. It's my supplier's problem

Making the problem someone else's won't work either. For a start, who are the suppliers involved? Most companies don't have an accurate inventory of all of the computer elements in their company — hardware, software, and all devices with computer chips. When they do conduct an inventory, they almost invariably find that they have far more computers and programs than they were aware of. Many systems are old; going back to the supplier of a computer that you bought two years ago and suggesting that it is the supplier's responsibility to make it year 2000 compliant is unlikely to meet with success. Many systems are too old and any warranties associated with their maintenance have expired or been allowed to lapse.

Even if the supplier is known and is responsible, it still doesn't mean that the work will be done. The supplier may not have the resources to apply to the problem, let alone the desire to accomplish the work which may have no revenue associated with it. More than a few commentators have already predicted a rash of bankruptcies of high-tech firms will be declared solely in order for a company to avoid incurring the costs associated with upgrading all of its existing software or hardware liabilities.

If a business had enough time, it might well be that it could partner with its suppliers to develop solutions, to find the optimum alternatives, to wait for that "silver bullet solution," or to slowly make the expenditures needed to replace old and outdated equipment. However, time is the one resource that is in finite supply, and it is decreasing with every rationalization made.

b. THREE REASONS WHY I DON'T WANT TO TELL MY BOSS

Unfortunately, even when someone recognizes the problem, there are some pretty strong reasons for being reluctant to take the message upstairs to senior management and advocating discussion at the next executive or board meeting. Most people don't want to be the bearer of bad tidings. In many offices, the "let's shoot the messenger" attitude is all too true. If that is the case, who wants to take the chance?

1. No compelling business rationale

The year 2000 issue may incur large cost and several years of work merely to bring a business system back to the stage it is at today (although it's two years to the deadline for mission critical systems, the work to connect *all* your programs won't stop then). Perhaps a company may be able to gather some considerable opportunities that can come with a comprehensive operational tune-up, and I discuss those later on. But initially the news will be that there is going to be a significant amount of extra dollars and time needed as a result of reviewing systems, with no obvious return.

Of course, no business has enough capital to do everything it wants. Even Microsoft, with billions in the bank, still selects its projects and investments and has budgets for each division to control spending. All business owners and managers make choices. Hopefully, they make the best possible choices among the options available.

The year 2000 problem leaves no choice: you will have to spend time dealing with it. When you go through the plan outlined in chapter 10, in Part III of this book, you will see that the process *must* draw time away from people's normal work schedules. You will be lucky if that is the only cost to the firm; it is highly probable that there will be a demand for dollars as well. For the majority of businesses, there are few, if any, tangible business benefits that will result.

The cost of converting systems to become compliant, or of merely protecting yourself from other systems that are not, is considerable. As long as there are skeptics within your company who won't believe that there is a need to spend the dollars in the first place, a proposal to spend thousands will often be regarded as throwing money away.

2. **Not a career-enhancing project**

Senior managers in a company usually earn promotion (and often substantial bonuses) based on the successful performance of their division or department. Success is usually based on comparisons with previous years' achievements. A senior information technology (IT) manager, faced with the costs of the year 2000 problem, can easily see his or her salary dropping radically over the next two or three years, along with the prestige and power that comes with the job.

On average, senior IT professionals last 18 months at any particular company before moving on. This means that these people are not likely to worry about the chaos they leave behind in any particular workplace. The temptation to ignore the enterprise's year 2000 concerns and move ahead on other projects is great.

3. **Lost opportunities**

Any time you expend on one area, you are *not* spending in another. Businesses have choices to make about where to invest their capital. Whether it is used to pay down debt, buy more inventory, open another branch or store, or invest in a marketing campaign, there are always competing demands on money. Typically, a manager or owner will decide where money should be spent by weighing the advantages of each choice. In the options above, the benefits of pursuing debt reduction could be reduced interest expense; buying more inventory could mean increased purchase discounts; a new branch might mean expansion into existing markets; or a new marketing plan might mean developing new markets.

All the time, effort, and money that you need to direct at the year 2000 problem will mean that money will be directed away from other options. Most of the time, we make our choices based on which projects will bring the most increased revenues and profits to the firm, or alternatively, reduce its expenses the most. The resources you spend on the year 2000 problem will be taken directly from other potentially profitable projects.

These examples of lost opportunities apply equally to large and small companies. Let us suppose that the person in charge of computers in your small enterprise comes to you, the senior manager. She tells you that instead of the usual $6,000 that you have been spending on computers each year, you are going to have to spend $25,000 for the next two years to replace all the PCs, the network, and all the software currently running on it. How will you receive this news? What if the employee bringing you this information is not a part of the senior management team? Computer support is often an intermediate position: are you going to listen to this person's recommendations? Will you choose to give up on some of the other programs being proposed for corporate expansion?

Finally, add to this mix the fact that this is a project in which the costs are almost impossible to predict and which are likely to increase from the original estimate.

- If you take three months to make your decision, and part of the plan is to hire some outside help, the costs of that help may well have risen substantially in the time it takes you to make the decision.

- You will probably find that you need to upgrade more software than was originally estimated and/or increase the software license fees you owe.

- Did the original estimate include the cost of your telephone PBX system, which you have just learned is non-Y2K compliant, and will crash on January 1, 2000?

c. TACTICS FOR DELIVERING THE MESSAGE

If you are the owner or president of a company, your concern may now be how to communicate the situation to your staff, customers, and vendors (see chapter 16). If you are a senior manager, you may want to consider the best way to get the message across.

You may want to convince one or more of your coworkers first so that the news you bring is from more than one person. You may want to start leaving articles about the year 2000 problem around your office in strategic locations. You may want to leave this or another book on the subject in the middle of the president's desk.

Yes, some of these tactics may be silly, and even worse — time consuming. But years of experience in the office world has taught me that there are many ways of bringing information to the attention of the appropriate decision-makers, and the frontal assault may not be the most productive. If you lose this battle, you may well lose the war as well, and that is something that neither you nor your business can afford.

4
PEOPLE PROBLEMS — PEOPLE POWER

Who is involved in the year 2000 problem? Everyone.

Although the problem is a programming glitch and an information technology challenge, the impact of the changes that will occur within an organization and the implications for its personnel, budgets, and other resources are comprehensive and universal, from the junior clerk to the president of the company and the board of directors.

Without support at all levels, any year 2000 initiative may be doomed to failure, and at best will be less than 100% successful. Once it's sold to top management, it requires absolute endorsement of the issue and their stressing its importance to overall company operations.

a. POSSIBLE ON-THE-JOB IMPACT

Table #1, found at the end of this chapter, outlines some of the ways that the year 2000 problem might affect more than 40 different jobs. Note that *all of these are the worst-case scenarios*. The idea is to give you a picture of the sorts of outside systems that could affect people's ability to work and the efficiency with which they handle a certain volume of activity.

About the only job I can think of that may not be affected by the year 2000 problem is a barber, who essentially operates with scissors, a razor, and a mirror. Even a hair stylist may have problems if he or she needs a hair dryer to operate and the power isn't on.

b. COMMUNICATION IS THE KEY

First and foremost, as many people as possible in the company must understand the problem and its related issues. This obviously extends beyond the computer department to all of a business's operations, such as accounting, sales and marketing, human resources, etc. A good first step is to read this book and gain a better understanding of the depth of the discussion that management needs to have with its staff. Chapter 16 outlines in more detail the overall communication plan you should consider.

Once you have drawn up the plan, communicate the issues to your staff as soon as possible. Inform all your staff and personnel about the issue and emphasize senior management's commitment to solving the problem. Point out that it is a universal one for the business, and let them know what the company plans to do and how all employees are involved.

Invariably, employees grow anxious when activity increases with no explanation from management. Even if you wish to downplay the specific impact that the problem might have on your business, you should still discuss the overall concept with employees so that they understand what the processes will be, and why some other projects may not be going ahead or will be delayed. Although this discussion will be ongoing, the earlier you start the communication process, the more time the business will have to successfully solve the problem.

c. COMPANY DIRECTORS

Company directors present a special case. These are usually a group of businesspeople and experienced professionals who have been invited to act as senior advisers to an organization. They work on behalf of shareholders, investors, management owners, and/or the general public to ensure that a company's affairs are run properly and with an eye to the enterprise's long-term benefit.

1. Responsibilities and liabilities

With the year 2000 crisis, the board of directors faces considerable responsibility and potential liability, both on a corporate and personal level.

First, as directors, they are responsible for the company's direction and management, both on a strategic and tactical basis. They are responsible for the company's long-term plans for itself, as well as ensuring that its management conducts itself responsibly on a day-to-day basis.

Their primary responsibility is to the company shareholders. This may extend beyond those who hold common shares to include investors who may hold shares, debentures, or other forms of rights against the company. The board of directors may also have a direct impact on the relationship the company has with its bank.

In addition, a director's actions, while not directly part of their responsibility, might have effects that will influence the direction or ownership of a company. For example, some shareholder agreements may specify the right of one shareholder to take over ownership from another in the event of actions that are detrimental to the overall financial health of the company. Ignoring the year 2000 problem would, in effect, trigger such clauses, because it holds considerable financial implications as well as potential effects on corporate operations. Were company directors to ignore the problem and make no recommendations as to what to do about it, they could be found to have neglected their responsibility to the company and to the shareholders.

Traditionally, directors who fail to live up to their fiscal responsibilities are not personally liable for a company's financial obligations, with the exception of outstanding wages. However, in the last two decades, particularly in the United States, there has been an increase in shareholders' suing fiscally irresponsible directors, including directors who make decisions that are not in the company's best interests.

"Lack of knowledge," a common defense against liability, will not be a viable argument as we get closer to the end of the century. The amount of information about the year 2000 problem will increase; any director who claims not to be aware of the significance of the problem will not be taken seriously. The "act of God" defense is also likely to fail. This is a problem caused by human failure with several years' advance warning. Directors cannot claim that it is a one-time, unexpected event with no recourse.

2. Defensive measures

J.P. Morgan Securities, one of the largest brokerage houses in the world, suggests that the best defense a director can have is to provide proof that he or she did the necessary homework toward becoming informed about the issues related to the year 2000 problem. The steps outlined below show what needs to be done. They also form the elements of a comprehensive plan that any company should draft in order to cover all the issues related to this impending crisis. This plan echoes what is explained in more detail in chapters 10 to 16. The point is that this plan should be drawn up and followed by the directors to prove their attention to their responsibilities.

(a) Put together a steering committee

The first step is to put together a committee to steer the company operations through each adjustment phase. This committee should include representation from all the departments, not just information technology and management. Senior executives should be involved, as well as users, technical personnel, financial staff, and perhaps outside consultants.

(b) Make a formal plan

A formal plan should be documented, but you should be prepared to revise it from time to time. New circumstances, developments, personnel, and purchases will affect its implementation. The basic elements of such a plan should cover all of the following:

(a) *Risk assessment and impact statement.* The first assessment that the company should undertake is an inventory of affected departments and systems. This includes all hardware and software, and may extend to machinery, inventory, and other items.

(b) *Communication plan.* A formal plan on how the company will communicate with its staff and with external customers and suppliers should be documented. As this will be an ongoing process, it is important that it be started as soon as possible. This will help establish early on that directors have taken a proactive attitude toward the year 2000 problem.

(c) *Budget.* A comprehensive budget should be established as early as possible. This will provide both the directors and company management with an idea of the funds required. Note that the budget should address both income statement and cash flow issues. Investments in hardware and software may place an unexpected strain on corporate finances unless well planned.

(d) *Critical path.* An overall timetable must be established in order to project what resources are needed, how they will be obtained, and how best to deploy them. This will be another tool to help management understand the implications of all the necessary actions that must be taken, and will probably emphasize how short the available time really is.

(e) *Appropriate documentation.* It is important to document all the decisions and actions of the steering committee as fully as possible. This documentation should include how the information is distributed internally and externally.

(f) *Status reports.* No plan will be set in stone. As changes take place, it is important that these changes be comprehensively documented and reported to appropriate personnel.

(g) *Investigation of alternatives.* Finally, the committee should ensure that it is pursuing all possible options for the best solution to the problem. Management could still be considered liable if they pursued a less than optimal course. Keep in mind that the board of directors may be faced with justifying its actions and opinions after the fact to a skeptical court that may not understand the limits of information available at the time of making a decision.

(c) Make the tough decisions

Since time is of the essence, all directors and senior management must recognize the time limitations inherent in the crisis, and make the best choices about the options to pursue. Concerns about quality, quantity, costs, resources, and deadlines will all have a bearing on what gets decided. There is no absolute requirement that directors make the correct decisions, but it is important that they demonstrate — and that they have documentation as backup — to prove that they based their decisions on the full information available at the time.

Management must show that it consistently solicited outside advice and searched for information to support its action plan. This includes attending year 2000 conferences and industry meetings, subscribing to relevant magazines and services, joining a regional or community task force, and attending trade shows to examine the latest year 2000 conversion software.

Company directors and management who follow a plan like this one will be able to make informed decisions and demonstrate that they took their responsibilities seriously and acted accordingly.

Chapter 10 discusses a year 2000 plan in more detail.

TABLE #1
YEAR 2000 IMPACT ON JOBS

JOB DESCRIPTION	IMPACT ON JOB
Accountant	Billing system inoperative; accounting system inaccurate or not functioning; slow down for receivables; inability to access cash
Airline pilot	Transportation system slow or broken; schedules not available; difficulties in international travel
Appliance repair technician	Huge increase in demand for services, but no spare parts; consumers angry; failure of some manufacturers
Bank teller	No information available on balances, checks, deposits, etc.; greater volume of cash transactions; longer lineups because ATMs don't work; need for longer hours
Banker	Financial systems broken; large increase in delinquent clients and bad debt provision; clients unable to provide accurate financial information; accounting system failures
Building superintendent	Internal systems failure (e.g., elevators, parking); increased demands for correction; potential loss of tenants
Bus driver	Schedules not available; dispatch system not working properly; traffic light problems; increased traffic jams; slowdowns in delivery capacity
Cab driver	Dispatch system not working properly; charge accounts not working; fewer business customers
Car salesperson	Increase in sales to replace failed systems, but angry customers; increased warranty claims; increase in sale of used (non-electronic) cars
Civil servant	Lack of information; systems not working; may have to deal with irate public who now lack services, money, etc.; potential changes in legislation, rules

TABLE #1 — Continued

Computer salesperson	Huge increase for replacement equipment; insurance claims/litigation
Construction worker	Shift schedules not available; problems with supply of materials
Cook	Unpredictable supplies, including lack of certain foods; delivery times less certain; some automated equipment won't work (particularly in fast-food restaurants)
Courier driver	Schedules not available; dispatch system not working properly; traffic light problems; increased traffic jams; slowdowns in delivery capacity
Customs officer	Failure of tracking systems and connections to police records; drop in amount of automated paperwork; increased traffic problems
Data entry clerk	Schedules not available; computer systems not working or refusing to accept date entry
Dispatcher	Schedules not available; dispatch system not working properly; traffic light problems; increased traffic jams; slowdown in delivery capacity
Doctor	Patient schedules and records not available; hospital admissions slowed; possible shortage of drugs (inventory problems)
Firefighter	Dispatch system not working properly; response times slowed; increased traffic jams; more false alarms
Gas station attendant	Failure of gas deliveries; cash register failure; credit card system failure; gas pump failure
Geologist	Equipment may not work; employers focus will be on fixing internal systems, not on new developments; analysis of samples slow because of transport problems; communications problems

TABLE #1 — Continued

Homemaker	Phone system not working; appliances breaking down; shortage of goods in stores; stores closed due to failure of systems
Importer/exporter	Phone system not working; exchange of goods, money, information between you and clients unreliable; big changes in markets means risks and opportunities
Insurance salesperson	Financial systems inaccurate; huge increase in loss of business claims; claims for broken equipment and corresponding workload; increase in litigation
Inventory clerk	Can't obtain inventory; can't get information about shipments; transportation system slow or broken
Lawyer	Litigation lawyers overly busy with suits and countersuits; clients can't pay; bankruptcies up sharply; real estate activity down
Machinist	Equipment not working; spare parts not available; inability to predict supply of materials and demand for finished product
Mail carrier	Increase in volume of regular mail; decrease in junk mail; traffic problems; failure in automated sorting systems
Management consultant	Phone system not working; computer system broken; photocopier broken
Manager	Phone system not working; schedules not available; office environment problems; computer systems inaccurate or not working
Mechanic	Large numbers of car systems failing; shortage of spare parts; electronic analysis equipment not working
Police officer	Dispatch system not working; response times slowed; increased traffic jams;

TABLE #1 — Continued

	increased robberies; increased false alarms; potential for violence due to frustrations
Politician	Angry consumers; increase in demands for intervention from consumers and businesses (bank foreclosures, credit rating errors, government checks); increased legislative action needed to try and manage crisis
Programmer	Huge demand for services; increased threats of lawsuits; blame for situation, personally and as profession
Real estate agent	Phone system not working; housing market down; traffic problems may change desirability of certain areas; downtown services suffering
Receptionist	Phone system not working; delivery service slow; photocopier not working
Restaurateur	Phone system not working; problem with food availability and deliveries; problems with payments by credit and debit cards
Retail sales clerk	Cash register not working; no credit card sales; bank unable to provide coin needed; increased potential for robbery (increased amounts of cash); decreased availability of inventory
Sales agent	Can't obtain inventory; can't get information about shipments; transportation system slow or broken
Secretary	Phone system not working; computer system not working, no word processing; photocopier not working
Security guard	Alarm systems not working; security passes invalid; phone system not working; increases in demand to replace failed automatic systems (parking, elevators, etc.)

TABLE #1 — Continued

Student	Schedule problems; loss of computer services within school; school bus problems (schedules, traffic)
Tax collector	Unreliable or no systems; large increase in underground economy, tax avoidance; possibly rapid changes in tax laws; many cash transactions unreported
Teacher	Class schedules not available; school computers not working; school bus transportation problems; difficulties in building systems may make classes difficult
Travel agent	Phone system not working; schedules not available; drop in volume of transportation capacity; drop in number of customers; difficulties in international travel
Truck driver	Schedules not available; dispatch system not working properly; traffic light problems; increased traffic jams; slowdown in delivery capacity
Waiter	Business slowdown means fewer customers; more cash business; credit card verification problems

5
TEAM EFFORT: KEEPING ALL DEPARTMENTS ON TRACK

It's time to look at the impact that the year 2000 will have on each department in your business. **Please note:** Even if your business has only two or three employees, don't skip this chapter! It may be that your organization relies on one individual to perform many "departmental" functions: regardless of size, the issues are common to almost all businesses.

Some aspects of this discussion may appear obvious, and, indeed, some companies will have developed all the necessary records — inventory, customer profiles, lists of assets — over the normal course of business. Companies that have these records have an advantage when it comes to solving the year 2000 problem, because it means that many inventories and processes that should have been documented in the past will continue to be documented now and in the future. This is the exception rather than the rule, however.

Two departments are more significantly affected than others: information technology and accounting. You may call them by different names, perhaps management information systems and bookkeeping, or their functions may be collectively called administration, but the operational elements remain the same. Let's look at those first. Other departments are discussed toward the end of this chapter.

a. INFORMATION TECHNOLOGY (IT)

The information technology (IT) department is the one most affected by this issue, and it will act as a natural focus for the year 2000 conversion. But don't make the mistake of leaving IT solely responsible unless the person in charge of this department has broad general management skills.

1. Inventory

The first step is providing a complete inventory of all hardware and software needs. Some managers will insist that they have this information already, but the inventory should be completed independently anyway. It will reveal that there is more hardware and software in use than would otherwise be shown by existing company records. If so, and it is likely, the limitations of existing documents and systems will be clearly demonstrated, along with the size of the problem.

The inventory should include all computers, phone systems, photocopiers, alarm systems, and any other devices and appliances that might have a computer chip embedded in their internal mechanisms. Whether this inventory is undertaken by the IT department alone or in cooperation with other affected departments is up to you. What's important is that the inventory be comprehensive and complete.

When documenting software, it is important to identify the various versions being used on different computers within the company. It's not enough to list only those legitimate copies of software contained in the company computer library; you must examine each individual computer to find out what is on its hard drive. It's not unusual for workplace computers to contain "unauthorized" software, either owned by the user or not recorded in the existing records of the company. Whether or not a company allows employees to install outside programs on workplace computers is one thing, but the important issue is that such programs may not perform properly on January 1, 2000, or may affect other programs with which they come in contact.

Your software inventory will help determine what is year 2000 compliant and what is not. You may find you don't have to replace all versions of your software, so your costs may be lower than first anticipated. The other value of this list will be to establish whether the company has purchased sufficient software licenses to cover the use of programs within the company. Software companies are becoming increasingly vigilant about pirated or copied software, and management is responsible for making sure that the company complies with all licensing agreements.

At the same time that this inventory is taking place, the IT department may also want to develop a list of all programs, such as spreadsheets, that depend on accurate date information in order to generate reports. IT may also develop its own date calculations for report purposes. Again, this will provide a better picture of the scope of the year 2000 problem within a business, and it may also give the company additional information about the best replacement programs to consider.

In addition to hardware and software assets, the IT department should also document the various systems that are in place that report on company operations. IT can do this or another department that operates independently. Links between systems should also be documented, as well as the chance to streamline or improve information flow.

2. Backup

Any company's computer operations should include regular backups. Unfortunately, many companies learn this the hard way — after a hard disk failure or other emergency. Ongoing backups are even more crucial within a year 2000 conversion, not only to maintain the most current set of corporate information, but also because a failure in amended programming code will mean restoring the previous set of "clean" code.

During your backup procedure, take careful note about the material being archived. Once any part of the conversion process has been completed satisfactorily, you may wish to back it up independent of the main company backups. Alternatively, once a portion of the conversion has been deemed acceptable, you may wish to go back and delete previous versions from backup tapes to ensure "bad" data cannot be mistakenly re-installed on the company's systems.

CAUTION! Entering an end-of-century date — December 31, 1999, 11:59 p.m. — and then waiting to see what happens when the internal clock reaches January 1, 2000, is one method talked about in the media as a way of identifying whether the CMOS chip in a computer is year 2000 compliant. The problem with this approach may be twofold. First, if the system cannot handle a 21st-century date, it may crash and make it difficult to retrieve any data in that computer. Alternatively, it may accept the date as changed, but it may also start to delete "old" files, since as far as it knows, these have been unused for two or three years. Sometimes these deletions can take place without the user being aware, or before he or she can stop it. Do a comprehensive backup before you try this test!

3. Software suppliers

The IT manager will have to watch out for software companies declaring bankruptcy in order to avoid having to upgrade older software to meet the new standards or to deflect potential lawsuits. This may affect the replace-versus-repair decisions for some systems.

4. Mergers and acquisitions

The year 2000 challenge will certainly bring some companies to the auction block. You should be on the lookout for them, because they represent substantial opportunities. It may even be that you can make exchanges with a potential partner that will benefit both of you (e.g., one company takes over both sets of manufacturing, the other both sets of distribution).

Your IT department will play a major role in such a merger or acquisition. Typically, you might not consult IT on such business transactions, at least not in the early stages, but now they have to be part of the analysis stage in order to assess the viability of integrating internal systems. Having IT's input from the start can help you avoid acquiring a company with an expensive year 2000 problem.

On the other hand, if their systems can easily be integrated into your present year 2000 plans, you may get an extra benefit out of the dollars you are already spending for your conversion.

5. Replacement costs and processes

The IT departmental budget will be absorbing huge extraordinary expenses. A typical company may replace 15% to 20% of its software each year. With a year 2000 conversion, a company may have to replace *all* of its software within two years. The same is true for hardware.

Quite probably, you will buy a great deal more computing power than the equipment you are replacing, in terms of speed and memory. But the costs of such replacement, although offering a far bigger bang for the buck than the original purchase, are still significant. And don't forget the cost of storage and archiving old material. It may also be necessary to re-enter a history of customer or supplier information to optimize purchases or sales.

b. ACCOUNTING

Next to the IT department, your accounting team is most likely to be substantially affected by year 2000 difficulties. As well, it faces a wider range of issues than merely inventory of systems and buying replacements.

1. Accounting systems

Let's start with the basics. The first item to check is whether your current accounting system can handle activities in the year 2000. This applies not only to data entry, such as invoice dates (incoming as well as outgoing) but also to the calculations related to those dates, e.g., the aging of accounts receivable and payable. This testing may be relatively easy to complete, although thorough backup is a must.

Great Plains is one of the few accounting packages that has already declared itself to be year 2000 compliant. Others will no doubt follow shortly. But check that it is *actually* compliant, not just *potentially* so. Each segment of whatever package chosen should be thoroughly tested in every possible way to eliminate all doubts that it can handle dates and calculations into the new millennium. Be sure to check billing, accounts receivable, accounts payable, payroll, and other date-sensitive issues, such as depreciation and amortization.

Depending on your company year end, the timing for a replacement, if necessary, may be critical. With a fiscal year end in early 1999, and a year's clean operation ahead of that, the amount of time left for researching your options, let alone the lengthy implementation process, is limited. (See chapter 13 for a full discussion.)

2. Financial history

The quality of a company's financial results reflects both its past business activities and its predictions for future operations. If the company's history is inaccurate, this will have a negative effect on any decisions about the future.

Many companies rely heavily on historical data, and much of that data may be carried in the accounting system. And it may not just be a question of summary sales or revenue figures. You may need detailed information on invoice numbers as well as precisely what was ordered and in what quantities.

Finally, if you are replacing your accounting system, "historical data" could be information that is less than one year old but retained on the old system. Ignoring or losing detailed data that is so recent could put you at a considerable disadvantage.

3. Audit

An audited set of financial statements represents a picture of a company's finances that is, in the auditor's professional opinion, fair and reasonable. The company auditor has a professional responsibility to bring significant financial and control-related risks to the attention of client management and board audit committees. Since the year 2000 problem represents a significant business risk, auditors will become increasingly vigilant in demanding to know the detailed plans being established to deal with this risk.

If, in the auditor's opinion, the steps being taken are inadequate to deal with the size of the problem, they may present you with a qualified audit, an audit flagged as not being in total conformity with generally accepted accounting principles (GAAP). This will have significant ramifications.

First, it could affect your relationship with your bank. Many loans are made on the basis of an unqualified audit, and if it is qualified in any way, the bank may withdraw its financing. At the very least, the cost of financing is likely to increase, the bank may demand further security, decrease the available line, or apply all three measures.

KPMG is one accounting firm that has established this list of questions that it now requires all its auditors to ask:

1. Has responsibility for year 2000 compliance been assigned to a senior executive?

2. Has a formal impact study been performed? What were the results?

3. Are the client's systems technologically interfaced with any of its suppliers, customers, or business partners?

4. Has the client confirmed that its major suppliers, customers, and business partners are year 2000 compliant?

5. Have any of the client's business partners requested confirmation of year 2000 compliance from the client?

6. What specific plans are in place to address the issues raised in the impact study?

7. What is the time horizon for putting those plans into action?

8. Does this client have archive data that is fundamental to its business?

9. How much does the client estimate that year 2000 compliance will cost?

10. Has the client factored year 2000 compliance costs into its budgets?

Audit questions courtesy of KPMG

Even if a company can successfully answer these questions, common concerns will be the cost of the time, effort, and documentation needed to prove its position. If a company cannot answer them to the auditors' satisfaction, there may be consequences at the company's bank, as well as with shareholders, investors, and the board of directors.

For some companies, a qualified audit statement may represent a significant problem if their shares are traded on a public exchange. Unqualified audit statements are usually required in most jurisdictions in North America, or at least a comprehensive set of documents must be filed to explain a variance from such unqualified statements. And while a qualification may have little immediate impact on a company, it will affect its attractiveness to investors in the long term, by sending out a signal that it is not managing obvious risks in an effective manner.

4. Budgets

Yet another major concern for the accounting department is the budget cost associated with year 2000 compliance. As stated previously, it is important that accounting calculate both the income statement impact *and* the effect on cash flow. Companies currently in the midst of year 2000 conversions show that initial estimates will almost invariably be too low. This will tend to throw a majority of costs into the last year of the century, 1999, and the impact on earnings in that year for publicly traded companies should not be underestimated. One financial commentator recently emphasized this point by saying that any company that says it has a precise idea of what its year 2000 costs will be, understands neither the implications nor the complications of the process.

In Canada, companies that use scientific research and educational tax credits (SREDs) in their research and development present a budgeting challenge. Departments engaged in R&D activities will also incur additional year 2000 costs. You may need to do some homework to ensure that future processes being developed by the company are year 2000 compliant.

The accounting department can begin by carefully analyzing the IT department's projections. Besides hardware and software costs, personnel costs must to be considered. One recent estimate suggested that $100,000 be set aside for each full-time member of the IT department.

Additional dollars should also be budgeted for outside consultants, and the figures for this may be even higher than IT personnel. The average daily rate for year 2000 experts in the United States is between $750 and $1,500 and is constantly rising. In one exceptional case in the United Kingdom, a consultant is receiving £4,000 a day, which is approximately U.S. $8,000. For the small business, there may be no need for this level of technical skill, but you may still need additional personnel, such as a part-time project manager, to assist with accounting system conversions.

5. Reporting the costs

One of the first rules I learned in Accounting 101 was that accounting is an art, not a science. Despite the fact that $1 + 1 = 2$, at the senior levels of accounting there is a large amount of judgment involved that can have a huge effect on financial statements. How these results are interpreted can, in turn, have an enormous effect on the value of the company, its share prices, and its relationships with its bankers and other investors.

For the non-accountant, the expenditure of monies to correct a problem related to the year 2000 problem would appear to be a straightforward reduction of the profit for that year. But in the world of accounting, when an expenditure is on something that has a useful life of more than a year, there is a generally accepted accounting principle (GAAP) that the cost should be spread over the period of time in which value is derived. So dollars spent on a piece of machinery, R&D, or investment in a particular project should be spread out over the life of that expenditure. For example, a piece of equipment that has a useful life of ten years and that costs $20,000 will be expensed via a depreciation cost that averages $2,000 a year. There are variations on this rule, but the general principle remains the same.

So what is the useful life of the money spent on a year 2000 conversion? From now until the year 2000? Beyond? What if the conversion also involves upgrading and re-engineering business processes? What is its useful life then? These questions are not merely arcane accounting rhetoric; they become real issues when you consider a company's bottom-line performance, particularly publicly traded companies.

Some of these accounting calculations are made on a judgment basis, others on rules drawn up by regulatory bodies, such as the Securities Exchange Commission (SEC) and the Canadian Institute of Chartered Accountants (CICA), or the American Institute of Certified Public Accountants. In both the United States and Canada, accounting associations are in the process of formulating rules for how expenses related to the year 2000 problem should be treated. At this time, it appears that the ruling will be that they should be written off as incurred, a significant hit to the bottom-line.

One additional problem may occur if the Canadian and U.S. stock exchange boards decide on different rules. Companies listed on a foreign exchange have long suffered under the difficulty (and cost) of having to report financial results in two different formats for two different bodies. There will be many Canadian companies operating internationally that will breathe a sigh of relief if the year 2000 bug does not cause yet another difference in financial reporting that must be accommodated.

Until these rules are decided and enforced, companies with identical operating results but different approaches to recording their year 2000 liabilities can appear to have completely different financial results, which may have broad implications. Given that investors like steady, predictable trends and may not understand the implications of the year 2000 problem, they might well make the wrong investment decisions based on what they believe to be "accurate" financial records.

Some of these reporting issues are being addressed. The various securities commissions and stock exchanges around the world will shortly have rules defining how companies should report their year 2000 costs. Auditors, too, may start to take a consistent approach as to how these dollars are reported on financial statements (see the above section on audits).

6. The banker's point of view

Bankers have long concentrated on a company's cash flow. While they usually demand audited financial statements to reassure themselves about the adequacy of the accounting systems and the fairness of the results being reported, they are also supremely interested in determining cash in and cash out. If cash flow is inadequate, they may deem your company "not bankable."

It is likely that banks will soon require companies to come up with a year 2000 conversion plan, as this will have a major effect on cash needs. Financing year 2000 plans presents a big drain on a company's resources, but unfortunately, it is all outflow with nothing coming back as inflow. This may mean an increase in the number of companies turned down for financing; some could even find their lines of credit canceled.

This will get the attention of your president and chief financial officer if nothing else will!

c. OTHER DEPARTMENTS

1. Manufacturing and production

An increasing amount of machinery and equipment, particularly on the production floor, comes with date-encoded chips as part of its integrated circuitry. Whether they are used for integration with order-entry systems, as links to computer-aided design programs, to guide lasers, or for robotics enhancement, they all help to make machinery and computers increasingly integrated. But even for a small company whose mechanical equipment has no electronics at all, the year 2000 problem needs to be examined. For example, a small manufacturing operation is likely to have machinery from a number of different countries, often European. If there is a slowdown or stoppage in the flow of spare parts for foreign equipment, the disruption it could cause to the company's production ability could be considerable. For such an enterprise, merely taking care to ensure that there are sufficient spare parts for four to six months of operation may be a simple solution.

Inventory control is another key management issue for production-oriented businesses. Many companies use a just-in-time (JIT) inventory ordering system that optimizes the company's use of its financial resources, but has some risk associated with it as well. With such a system, the failure of a single supply in the early part of the year 2000 may close down the entire operation. For some industries, such as automobile production, there is enormous concern over such an event because if a single crucial part fails to arrive, it could close down the entire production line.

You can take a few steps now to avoid potential problems. First, communication now with your suppliers is crucial. Are they prepared for year 2000? Second, you might want to start gradually increasing your raw material stocks. The balancing act required will depend on the specifics for each company, and there are no absolute rules. To work out the best solution, the production department will have to work more closely than ever with the IT and accounting departments.

2. **Purchasing**

An assured source of supply is important for a company's long-term operations planning and an integral part in the selection of reliable suppliers. Over the next two years, purchasing agents will have to spend an increasing amount of time determining that the purchases they are about to make are from a year 2000 compliant company. And not only will they be doing this to guarantee their own source of supply, but they may be under increasing pressure to demonstrate to their own customers that they themselves are a compliant source.

Finding new suppliers is never a quick and easy process, so it should be started as soon as possible. In some industries there may only be a few suppliers that can guarantee delivery in early 2000. This state of affairs will, of course, drive prices up, so another advantage of starting the search early is that it may establish you as a long-term customer who merits more attractive terms.

Finally, purchasing will be required to evaluate currency fluctuations more carefully to protect against adverse changes. Some governments' failure to deal with the year 2000 problem may place the foreign currencies and overseas suppliers at greater risk than normal. (An expanded discussion of this topic is included in chapter 9.)

3. **Sales and marketing**

In many small- and medium-sized enterprises, the sales staff has, by its own preference, as little as possible to do with either computers or accounting. The year 2000 problem demands a change in this attitude, because these people are in the front line of identifying potential customers and often are the best intelligence sources on competitors' shortcomings. From a financial point of view, customers who fail to address the year 2000 problem run the risk of being unable to pay their bills in early 2000. In this respect, they are as serious a threat to the company's financial well-being as a supplier's failure to deliver enough inventory material.

Salespeople are often reluctant to evaluate a new customer's credit rating and prefer to leave that task to the accounting department. But the state of a company's year 2000 readiness is more than a simple answer to a simple question. Errors in judgment in this respect will raise major risks for a business if not handled properly. For this reason, sales staff may have to undertake more investigation than merely obtaining an order.

4. Personnel and human resources

On the surface, the problems related to year 2000 staffing issues are relatively simple:

(a) to find appropriate resources,

(b) to keep them, and

(c) to pay them enough.

These issues will continue to be dealt with primarily by technical personnel, but project management and other expert help may also be needed. Pressures may come from unexpected sources, such as older, established, loyal employees with a knowledge of COBOL who may find the prospect of high daily rates for the next two years attractive enough to quit their present secure positions and go freelance.

Finding technical employees is becoming increasingly difficult, even without the added complication of year 2000. It may be that you do not need personnel with any special year 2000 skills, but you may still be affected by an ever-increasing rate of pay across many other industries. Bonuses may also be demanded. If possible, you should avoid paying regular bonuses and try and keep technical staff motivated with a bigger bonus to be paid in the year 2000. You may also wish to consider non-monetary compensation in the form of shares or other perks.

It is likely that the rate of pay for technical skills will cause comment and resentment from other employees, who may be equally trained but in relatively low-demand functions. Unfortunately, there are no easy human resource solutions for accommodating the year 2000 problem.

5. Office operations

It should come as no surprise that even the administrative functions of a small business will be affected by the year 2000 problem. This is an area where many company functions intersect, even if in apparently mundane and repetitive tasks. Because of this integration, it may be that an administrative assistant will spot problems that affect several departments that they may have missed themselves.

Administration is also the department that often is responsible for the design and ordering of forms for all kinds of corporate functions. For the last 50 years, many such forms have had their century dates inserted automatically. For example, almost any check you examine has a blank line for the month and for the date, but the year is printed as 19___. Monitoring the company's use of forms like this is essential; it's another area where errors can be made and additional expenses incurred.

6. Retail

If your business involves a retail element, it is here that you will have to deal with the year 2000's consequences for your customers.

First, you may have equipment that doesn't work. If this includes your credit card or debit card reader, you will be unable to process those sales because you won't be able to establish whether the customer can charge anything.

Or the problem may be just the reverse if your cash register doesn't work. If this is the case, you may still be able to process the sale, but you will rapidly lose track of all of your automated inventory systems. Make sure, too, that your sales clerks have the basic math skills to make correct change. (If you don't think that this is a valid concern, just watch what happens today when a store has a temporary electricity blackout. Many tellers cannot do the basic addition and subtraction necessary to make correct change.)

Plan too for the fact that you will be handling more cash in the early part of the year 2000. If credit and debit cards become unreliable and you are unable to verify checks, you will be left to deal with more cash. You may have to look at better cash control procedures as well as security issues, such as robbery prevention.

Finally, make sure you have inventory to sell. The millennium bug may cause huge problems with transportation systems, especially with overseas suppliers. If your store normally carries only a 15- to 30-day supply of inventory, you may need to reexamine this policy. Even though you should usually minimize your investment in inventory, it will be much better to have inventory that you can eventually sell than a perfectly working operation with nothing on the shelves.

7. Facilities management

Embedded chips potentially pose a far greater problem for businesses than computer systems. Buildings and their systems and equipment are a major location for chips. Just think of some of the systems affected:

(a) *Parking control.* Typically equipment controls building passes or issues parking tickets for visitors. If this system fails to operate correctly on January 1, 2000, it will contribute at the least to irritation and confusion, and in the worst case will cause considerable backups and contribute greatly to overall traffic chaos.

(b) *Security.* Current systems are designed to recognize security passes, but at the start of the millennium, security systems may not be working, or could work erratically depending on the date embedded in the security card itself. Even if the overworked security guard has the time available, he or she may not be able to follow the alternative method of telephoning for permission to clear a visitor because the phone system itself may be unusable or unreliable.

(c) *Elevators.* Elevators have a date-encoded chip to assist in their operation and many also have an interrelated security system built in. If the elevators interpret January 1, 2000, as a Monday (which was the day on January 1, 1900) instead of Saturday, which it is, the elevators may provide limited operation, require all users to have appropriate security cards, or even fail to function at all.

(d) *Heating, ventilation, and air conditioning.* These systems have become increasingly complicated over the years, shunting heat from one part of the building to another, sensing outside air temperature and turning systems on and off, even monitoring air quality to make sure that it is acceptable. Just like anything else with date-encoded chips, they pose a risk of breaking down or being unreliable.

If you have a department or staff to deal with facilities, make sure they are involved in your year 2000 plan. If you are on the 50th floor of an office building and your computer systems are working perfectly, but the elevators are locked in position on the ground floor, your company's operations will be stalled too.

d. SUMMARY

This chapter is a red flag to stress to you the all-encompassing impact of the year 2000 problem and how the actions of one department, even a department as important as information technology or accounting, will not by themselves solve the issues for the company as a whole. The deliberate strategy of senior management must be to emphasize their top-down support for all year 2000 corrective activities and to encourage input from everyone to help address all of the company's operational concerns.

This, too, is why the single coordinator managing all year 2000–related activities needs to have a comprehensive understanding of all your company operations, and not be focused on a single division or department. Without such an individual, the broadly based steering committee will have to take on the task of ensuring that *all* responsibilities and accountabilities are being dealt with.

6
IT'S A LEGAL MATTER

Few companies have a full-time legal adviser on staff, but all will be familiar with a range of legal issues that they need to deal with every day. It comes as no surprise that the year 2000 programming issue will complicate the legal affairs of any company, as well as the costs involved.

One estimate of completing the programming changes required for 600 billion lines of code at $1 per line is $600 billion. The legal fees associated with this process may reach *$3 trillion*, an almost unimaginable amount. This estimate may be high for Canada, where litigation is less common, but even a fraction of that estimate is astonishingly high.

a. DIRECTORS' AND OFFICERS' LIABILITY

You and your company lawyer should discuss the potential liability of your directors and officers. For a small- to medium-sized business, directors liability might be considered in the context of individual shareholder and/or investors agreements. In a number of instances, there may be clauses in a shareholder agreement related to fiscal responsibility and reporting. If they are not followed, it may trigger other results, such as an option to buy out shares or to acquire control of a company. So even a director of a small firm needs to be aware of year 2000 issues and how they will affect the company. (See chapter 4 for more discussion on directors' liability.)

b. MERGERS AND ACQUISITIONS

If you are considering buying a company whose operations complement your own, one of your highest priorities will be to examine its computer systems and determine whether they are year 2000 compliant. If they are not, you may incur significant costs in adjusting and upgrading them.

A purchased company's disclosure of its state of year 2000 preparedness is a legal concern. If the selling company does not disclose to the buyer the risks and liabilities associated with that aspect of the sale, it could be held liable for misrepresentation and possibly be sued.

Ignorance may not be a valid defense in any court case considering the matter in 1999 or later.

c. COPYRIGHT

Medium-sized companies usually do not use off-the-shelf software. Often they will have developed many of their own systems based on an application that they bought a number of years ago. That software vendor may have insufficient resources to upgrade the application, and that may force the company to do it on its own. But it may not have that right! Buying the application may not give it the right to modify the source code and, in theory, the software vendor could sue at a later date for infringement of copyright.

As the deadline draws nearer, more businesses will be prepared to do *anything* to ensure their business operations are working into the new millennium. In this atmosphere, more violations of copyright are likely to occur even if they are unwitting. If you have any doubts, you should consult your lawyer.

> Currently, there is a case pending in Canada in which a company has copyrighted the phrase "Year 2000" and has legal action against another company manufacturing items with this phrase stamped on it.

---

d. CLASS ACTION SUITS

Larger institutions, particularly those involved in the financial community, may face class action suits from groups of shareholders, investors, or consumers. Imagine an insurance company whose systems crash and lose information related to life insurance policies held and payouts to beneficiaries. Or imagine a similar company whose computers produce erroneous results in the calculations of benefits or annuities. Consider too the case of an investment firm that has made investments in companies that were not year 2000 compliant. A strong argument will be made that the firm was negligent in not considering the liabilities and risks associated with such an investment.

Another possibility is a group legal action against a bank whose failed systems cause other businesses to go bankrupt through the domino effect, especially if such businesses were financially strong on December 31, 1999.

These and other types of class action suits are likely to be common in the year 2000 and beyond. Whether there will be any assets to pay off the damages sought is another matter, but there is little doubt that the courts will be kept very busy solving these legal issues for a number of years to come.

e. DISCLOSURE OBLIGATIONS

From a legal point of view, disclosure involves the accurate representation of the company's circumstances in letters to customers. Many form letters are starting to appear from customers to suppliers to confirm their readiness for the year 2000. In many cases, the suppliers are signing these and returning them with very little understanding of the legal issues involved and the potential liabilities of what could be considered misrepresentation. Often they have limited knowledge about whether their own suppliers can provide compliant goods and services, a factor that naturally influences their own quality control.

f. CONTRACT LIABILITIES

Imagine a situation where a company is unable to deliver engine parts contractually on time because its computer software failed. Apart from the lawsuit that may come from the customer for failure to perform, the supplier might sue the hardware manufacturer for supplying a product with a known "defect," or sue the software supplier that installed programs without checking for compliance, or both. The software supplier might even sue the hardware company because it relied on its technical department's statements that the equipment was year 2000 ready — and so on and so on. Lawsuits like these ones are already taking place in 1997!

> Stephen Brower, a U.S. lawyer specializing in year 2000 issues, has identified the following potential defendants in possible contract litigation:
> - Software vendors of non-compliant systems

- Year 2000 consultants/solution providers
- Software acquisition consultants
- Year 2000 "certification" entities
- Software vendors of compliant systems (the rush to install will create deficiencies and unmet expectations)

So there will be an increasing amount of legal involvement when drawing up contracts. You may wish to insert some year 2000 paragraphs in contracts with suppliers, or you may be asked to endorse similar paragraphs in contracts from your present customers. Such clauses can range from the benign to the ridiculous, and the penalties may be extreme if you are unable to perform to the letter of the contract. Note too that a company may in fact be penalized for losing a contract where it is *not* prepared to sign unreasonable year 2000 clauses. In this case, even if you avoid future penalties, you may be hit hard in short-term sales losses.

g. TAX CONSIDERATIONS

A few months ago, I heard the comment that in 1999 the United States would move to a flat tax system. At that time I thought the remark was a joke, but I'm not so sure anymore. In early 1999, the United States may be faced with two choices: to either install a very simple tax system that can be easily designed and implemented within a nine-month period, or not collect any tax at all.

Whether or not this actually comes to pass, it won't really matter whether you consider tax a matter for your lawyers or for your accountants. In either case, there is little doubt that the year 2000 problem will provide more complications for your tax preparations and more work for both these groups of professionals.

1. **Domestic tax law**

It is still unclear how the tax authorities in various countries will treat one-time expenses related to solving the year 2000 problem. The Financial Accounting Standards Board (FASB) in the United States has stated that such expenditures are to be expensed in the year incurred. This will have a considerable effect on income statements, and if carried through at the tax level, a reduction in the amount of tax payable to the government. Many companies already have to deal with differences between income reported for tax purposes to a state or a province and the income calculation for a federal government. This may make it yet more complicated.

Until all the rules and regulations related to this aspect of the millennium bug are resolved, this concern will still be a work-in-process. Even if the United States and other countries move to a flat tax rate, rules related to the transition between the two systems will still make the domestic tax regime very complicated for the next several years.

2. **International tax aspects**

The rules for trading between international partners is sure to become more complicated. Over the years, various rules have been established to ensure that profits are not artificially transferred from one jurisdiction with high taxes to another with low taxes as a means for a large corporation to minimize its taxes and pay less than its fair share. Now if a parent company undertakes a program to make sure that all of its systems are year 2000 compliant, and runs that program from its head office in Canada or the United States, it could face substantial tax problems defining where the costs and benefits are "deemed" to have occurred.

Tax lawyers look out — there's plenty of business heading your way!

PART II

THE BIG PICTURE — GOVERNMENT, INFRASTRUCTURE, AND THE BANKS

7
WHAT'S BIG BROTHER UP TO?

a. THE ROLE OF THE FEDERAL GOVERNMENT

The role that government has to play in helping resolve the year 2000 crisis is twofold:

(a) First, it must fix all of its own systems.

(b) Second, it should act as a leader in ensuring that everyone else is aware of the problem and provide whatever help is necessary to access the resources so that their systems can also be corrected.

1. Internal government systems

Given the size of government today and its involvement with all aspects of our daily life, it will come as no surprise that the organization with the biggest year 2000 problem is the government itself.

Many government systems are based on a legacy of policies and procedures that have been developed over decades. Since so much government work is based on precedent, it is relatively rare that a department will decide to redesign and reprogram its computer systems from scratch. In Canada, for example, a couple of major policy changes, particularly the introduction of the goods and services tax (GST) and the signing of the North American Free Trade Agreement (NAFTA), did prompt a major rewrite of the federal government tax programs. For this reason, some of the government programs in Canada are more advanced from the perspective of year 2000 than in other countries. Nevertheless, the size of the task is still huge.

Both the U.S. and Canadian governments insist that all of their departments are fully aware of the problem, that plans have been made to correct original programming or replace it with new programs, and that all of their respective operations will be year 2000 compliant by the time the new millennium arrives. Certainly, some departments are well advanced and will meet the deadline with time to spare. Others, however, are not nearly as advanced as the government's official position would like to portray.

The size and scope of this book does not allow a full discussion of every government department. But in this chapter, I concentrate on three ministries and departments that are most likely to affect the economic operations of small- and medium-sized businesses in North America.

You should also keep in mind any other departments that you deal with for your own specific business. For example, environmental concerns may influence your production processes, government statistics may influence your next consumer campaign, and foreign affairs may deal with your overseas markets. Whatever you do, you *cannot* afford to assume that they are all up to speed on the issue, and you *mustn't* believe all of their assurances about how everything will be fine without probing more deeply and hopefully finding some support for their affirmations. You cannot afford to risk your business on the political reassurances of a government bureaucrat.

2. Taxation

The core of any government financial system is the collection of tax revenue. In Canada, initial reports suggest Revenue Canada is well advanced in its conversion program. The size of its mandate, however, is daunting, and I know of at least one individual responsible for the program who has been ordered by his doctor to take an extended rest from the stress caused by the size of the task and its uncompromising deadlines.

The United States faces a greater challenge because the systems of the Internal Revenue Service (IRS) have not undergone the recent renovation seen in the Canadian systems (caused by GST and free trade legislation). The IRS also started working on the problem later in the game, and so its deadlines are correspondingly tighter. The IRS is also looking at whether it should repair or replace its systems, or do a combination of both.

> In a recent issue of the Information Technology Association of America's newsletter, it was reported that when the Chief Information Officer of the IRS was asked about the challenge of trying to balance the repair/replace equations, his response was to compare this situation with a scene from the movie "Butch Cassidy and the Sundance Kid." When the two outlaws are hesitating to jump from the side of a canyon into the river, Butch is reluctant, explaining that he can't swim. Sundance tells him not to worry

as the fall will probably kill them both in the first place. What a choice!

A huge challenge facing the tax departments in both Canada and the United States is how to deal with outside organizations and their systems. The tax department does not have the option of accepting or rejecting data received from these bodies, but must work with it in order to integrate it into their existing systems. Not only must the department encourage all these organizations to upgrade their own systems to become year 2000 compliant, it must also be able to detect information that is incorrect and adjust it so that it can be entered into its own system without causing any damage. Think about what that means: if the tax department receives information that is not compliant, it must identify that information as such, segregate the data, correct it, and re-integrate it into the tax collection systems. And as David Archer of Revenue Canada says of the 180,000 businesses with which Revenue Canada deals, "most of them are unwilling participants."

The federal government in Canada must also be integrated with the provincial government systems so that transfer payments and the provincial share of tax revenues are accurately distributed. The state and federal governments in the United States are less integrated, but the amount of information transferred between the two systems is still considerable.

3. Customs and transportation

Much of the world's international trade depends on the ability of goods to cross international boundaries speedily and efficiently. This process may be made easier in free trade zones, such as the European Union or the North American Free Trade Area, but whether or not any customs duties and revenues are collected, it is as important that there be as little delay as possible in the open movement of goods and people.

Computers are increasingly used to track all kinds of transport, from airplanes to ships and trucks, and even cars. A large amount of this tracking uses satellite technology to keep track of the locations of millions of vehicles.

Most small businesses have come to take this movement for granted. Whether supplies come from across the street or from the other side of the globe is increasingly irrelevant to most businesses, provided that they can get the correct amount in the right time frame at the best price. If these systems should break down, however, the whole equation will change drastically.

One immediate area of concern is air transport of both goods and people. The Dutch airline KLM has stated that it will refuse to fly certain routes in early 2000 if it believes that the safety control systems on those flights will not be comprehensive enough to guarantee passenger safety.

While stories of airplanes dropping out of the sky at one second after midnight on January 1, 2000, are probably exaggerations, a much more realistic scenario is that due to a failure of some systems, airplanes will be unable to take off in the first place. Corporation 2000, a firm that specialized in predicting the broader impact of year 2000 failures in a wide geographic area, suggests that no airplanes will leave the Gatwick and Heathrow airports in London, England, for a month before January 1, 2000, as well as for a month afterward.

Even if you assume that any disruption to world transport control systems is only temporary, your business will have to adjust by ensuring it has adequate inventory in stock on December 31, 1999. This inventory may be materials for production, objects for resale at a retail or wholesale level, spare parts for machinery and equipment, or all of the above. Companies planning to ship or order goods at the end of 1999 should investigate alternatives and consider their options.

Delays in transportation may not be confined to physical systems. Much of the commerce conducted today involves a considerable amount of electronic communication, if in fact commerce doesn't consist entirely of electronic transfers. Businesses should recognize that if one element in the entire chain breaks down, the sale will fail, or at best, payment may be considerably delayed. The failure could come from a financial institution, customs broker, telecommunication system, or from some other small element in the system. If overall systems within a particular country are sufficiently disrupted, temporary restrictions may be placed on the transfer of funds.

At this stage, the cash flow aspects of making overseas sales will become very important. Even if you can land a lucrative contract at the end of 1999, you should be very certain that you can collect payment on it, as the cash flow risk to your business may be considerable. Letters of credit or bank drafts may help, but I anticipate that there will be an increasing amount of invoices factored at the end of the century, the broker being prepared to undertake the risk, albeit at a significant discount.

I recognize that many of the previous comments are not directly the responsibility of government. However, national governments are usually heavily involved in different aspects of controlling and/or taxing transportation. Organizations such as the Federal Aviation Authority (FAA) for the control of air traffic, Canadian and American customs officials and port authorities, and regulations about the safe movement of goods are just some of the dozens of other areas where government is involved. The question remains as to whether the government will be part of the problem or part of the solution when it comes to untangling the transportation mess in which we are liable to find ourselves.

4. **Social security and welfare**

Social security covers a huge range of programs, including pensions, medical payments, unemployment, welfare, child assistance, living subsidies, day care assistance, training assistance — the list goes on and on. Many businesses cater to specific segments of the population that receive these forms of social assistance, and many individuals depend entirely on the arrival of that government check once a month.

When the U.S. government was shut down for a period in 1996, economists were able to track the drop in economic activity when all kinds of government checks failed to arrive on time. A disruption in this economic flow would cause major economic changes both locally and nationally.

The big concern I have is that the social security departments deal with the most needy part of our society. Government officials say they are on track to fix their systems in time. However, in the United States, the Social Securities Administration has recently admitted that in addition to the 30 million lines of proprietary code that it is trying to fix, it has just "discovered" an additional 33 million lines of related code installed by outside vendors also needing mediation. Meanwhile, in Canada, there was a news story about contingency plans to issue welfare checks by hand if need be!

These are government areas over which we individually have little control and influence, but which have immense impact on the lives of millions of Canadian and U.S. citizens. Certainly both national governments insist that they will not let any portion of the population suffer through failure of any critical systems because of the year 2000 problem. I truly hope that they succeed.

b. STATE AND PROVINCIAL GOVERNMENTS

Like the federal government, state and provincial governments also influence many aspects of business life. The areas most likely to affect small- and medium-sized enterprises are the transportation department, the court system, and the office or department in charge of employment standards.

1. Transportation

It is interesting that all three levels of government, federal, state or provincial, and municipal, control some aspects of the transportation system. It is also perhaps a little worrisome. It will be an enormous task to try to coordinate the year 2000 corrections of hundreds of businesses involved with transport to ensure that this complicated and vital system does not fail on January 1, 2000. It will become more complicated by the fact that governmental authority is also split between three levels.

The largest area of activity for provincial or state governments is probably licensing cars and trucks. Millions of these licenses are issued and renewed each year and, indeed, millions of people who make their living from driving vehicles depend on the safe and prompt arrival of cars or trucks. A number of states have already encountered problems with licenses extended to the year 2000 disappearing from computer systems. And the problem for small business will arrive whether the system fails or even if the process of issuing licenses slows down dramatically.

In a recent news article, officials from the Ontario Ministry of Transport admitted that they were running into problems due to an inability to show registration renewals to be issued in 1998 for the year 2000. The ministry has refused an offer of a financial contribution from the Used Car Dealer's Association to hire more programmers to solve the problem. "You can only get so many mechanics under the hood," quipped a ministry official.

Alamo Rent A Car encountered this problem way back in 1981 when it tried to enter British drivers' licenses (which are good for 20 years) and found that their system couldn't handle the date.

The same system for licensing and registration of vehicles is integrated with those for traffic violations. Beyond that, it feeds information into police systems and enables them to track items such as stolen vehicles. While you may wish that some of your parking tickets would drop off a government system, you hardly want drunk or dangerous drivers to be able to drive in your community with impunity, knowing that their records cannot be accessed and that they are unlikely to be caught.

Date problems may also affect the computer records on safety-related matters. In Ontario, there has been an alarming increase in the number of accidents involving trucks, particularly with lost wheels. The Ontario government has launched an aggressive campaign to combat this problem, assisted by the provincial trucking association.

From a small business point of view, the licensing systems date problems may be important for a variety of reasons. Do you hire drivers and need to confirm what type of license they have, or the quality of their driving record? Do you own vehicles in the company whose licenses you need to renew? Do you have other licenses you need to get in order to continue your business, such as ones that allow you to operate in another province or state? Or are your insurance rates based on clean, accident-free records being provided to the insurance company?

Many states and provinces are also major contributors to the development and operation of mass transit systems. While these may be less important to the direct operation of your business, they will naturally be of prime concern to employees who use them to get to work. Public transit systems will be vulnerable to year 2000 problems in the areas of fuel supply, electric power, and scheduling systems. On the other hand, if they are working well, they may also be overloaded trying to transport the possibly thousands of people who will have had to abandon their cars that won't function because of problems at the start of the new millennium.

2. The court system

Most small- and medium-sized enterprises deal with the court system fairly regularly, generally on issues concerning traffic offenses, unpaid bills, or contractual disputes. And the court system is a bureaucracy that is highly dependent on computer systems, just like any other organization.

In many jurisdictions, the courts already have a huge backlog. The tremendous workload that the courts are trying to handle means that it can take years before a case reaches the bench. A simple 15-minute court appearance can cost a whole day of waiting, and many small businesses are reluctant to get involved in the legal process because they cannot afford the time involved. If court scheduling processes were to break down and cause even more delays, it would be bad news indeed.

3. Employment standards

The year 2000 problem may raise a whole new set of issues related to employment standards and labor law. If a company lays off workers for a month because of delays in the delivery of raw materials or parts from a company whose computer systems fail, will labor laws be applied in exactly the same way as in other business circumstances? Extended layoffs usually require a company to give notice and some union contracts may not allow them at all. Unemployment benefits are often based on whether the worker is unemployed or laid off. With year 2000 problems, neither employee nor employer may know how long the delay will be.

The Gartner Group has predicted that between 1% and 10% of businesses may fail worldwide as a result of the year

2000 crisis. This means that thousands of people will suddenly be out of work. A natural consequence would be an immediate rise in the number of claims against former employers for compensation according to the labor statutes in place. The whole system might then be at risk from a combination of scheduling problems, the sheer volume of cases, the ability of companies or individuals to pay the penalties involved, and even whether the year 2000 cases would be heard under the same set of rules as other labor disputes.

c. MUNICIPAL GOVERNMENTS

As you move down the hierarchy of governments to those more concerned with local issues from those with the responsibility of overseeing the national scene, the awareness of the year 2000 problem decreases. The implications of this ignorance are considerable, as it is these systems that may have the first impact on consumers and businesses in the initial part of the new century.

1. Traffic control

Traffic light systems and all forms of traffic control are usually the responsibility of local governments. Consider the economic implications of large-scale traffic chaos in cities such as Toronto, Chicago, or Dallas if these systems do not work in the early part of the next century. In effect, we could wake up to cities that have no traffic control systems at all. New York experienced this scene 100 years ago, before the advent of traffic lights, and there were enormous traffic snarls as hundreds of carriages and carts tried to negotiate the streets. With the increased number of vehicles on the road today, the problem would be many times worse.

> In an unusual experiment in Phoenix in 1994, a date in the year 2000 was entered into the traffic system to see what, if any, impact this would have. The

entire system crashed and stayed down for three days. That system has now been made year 2000 compliant, but at a cost of over $63 million and the expenditure of a considerable amount of time.

2. Water and waste management

Municipal governments are also responsible for managing the water that comes out of your taps every day. This may include collecting it in dams, pumping it to your community, and storing it in reservoirs and then eventually pumping it through your pipes. The same system organizes the collection of the dirty water, as well as sewage, and sends it to the treatment plant. When it is clean it is released back into the water system. Sometimes the same water is reused many times in different communities as it moves downstream.

There is considerable risk that one of the components may not work correctly on January 1, 2000. Water systems are more electro-mechanical than electronic, and may be somewhat less susceptible to failure than the electrical system. Many have embedded chips built into their core operations. But they still carry the problems of any large integrated system: if one component shuts down, the whole system may be unable to carry on. And if there are any breakdowns, health risks could arise from improperly treated water.

3. Fire, police, and ambulance

The computer systems that emergency departments rely on are usually highly sophisticated and linked with others across the region and country. These systems and services face three distinctive problems not common to others: information services breakdown, failure of automated systems, and increased volume of crime.

(a) Information systems

Because all sectors of our society are subject to crime, the information systems police use have connections to all kinds of data in every type of industry all over the world. The police also have their own internal systems for recording criminal records and evidence as well as correlating information collected from all the other sources.

Police operations would be severely hampered by the failure of any part of the overall network, ranging from their dispatch systems and general communication to scheduling and record keeping.

Fire and ambulance services often rely on sophisticated systems to tell them where an alarm is coming from and what is the quickest route to take.

For all emergency services, speed is of the essence. If the systems that facilitate that rapid response break down or even slow down, human lives are literally at stake.

(b) Failure of automated systems

As crime levels have increased many of us have turned to private services and automated systems for protection. The size of these services outstrips the size of public resources in some regions. They depend on automated cameras, alarm systems, automatic dispatch calls, and other methods to cover the 99% of uneventful monitoring, as well as identify the 1% where a security response is required. This monitoring may extend to such mundane systems as parking access and elevator passes.

All these security systems include date chips or programs with dates so they can pinpoint the exact time of any given event, which means they are vulnerable to year 2000 problems. If they fail, more demand will be placed on people to deal with the situations that have in the past been monitored by machines.

(c) More crime

Very likely, the year 2000 will bring with it an increase in crime. Bank vaults are liable to start opening on Saturdays when the date chip buried in the door tells them it is Monday. (The first day that this will happen is on Saturday, January 1, 2000.) More cash being used in financial transactions because of credit and debit card failure and the unreliability of checks could mean more robberies. Failed building systems will invite more property crime and layoffs. Traffic problems and financial woes will lead to more personal stress — and more domestic and other violence.

4. Financing the costs

Where will the money come from to finance all the necessary changes? This is a question all levels of government must ask — and answer — but municipal governments may be the hardest hit. Municipal budgets are smaller and have less room to move funds around.

d. GOVERNMENT READINESS

The state of preparedness varies considerably from government to government and country to country. Contact any department that is of concern to you or your business and ask your own questions. That way, your planning (or lobbying) can be focused in the right areas. Keep in mind, however, that most government spokespeople are going to claim readiness in order to avoid any kind of public relations mess. Alternatively, the department official may not know the true state of readiness.

At the federal level in Canada, considerable progress has been made, and the government is probably on track in most cases to convert most of the major systems. I am considerably more skeptical abut the progress being made in the United States. One commentator has suggested that the U.S. federal government is doing a masterful job — on the public relations front — but that the actual progress in converting the technology is considerably more in doubt.

Some state and provincial governments have the situation well in hand and have comprehensive, well-funded plans. Others show a lack of planning and resources, or worse, have hardly recognized the problem at all. Major municipalities are addressing the problem, but many rural communities are often unaware that the problem even exists.

Whether we like it or not, much of our economic well-being is tied up with the efficient operation of governments at all levels. As a small businessperson, you should be aware of what aspects of your business could be affected by any shutdown of government activities and protect your business accordingly. Spend as much time as possible putting pressure on governments to deal with the problem, and encourage you neighbors and associates to do the same. Time is our worst enemy in this matter, and the more time wasted protecting misguided bureaucrats, the less time there is to fix the problem or prepare proper contingency plans.

8
THE TIES THAT BIND: LOOKING AT THE INFRASTRUCTURE

Those large companies that provide our businesses with daily power, heating, water, and communications — collectively known as utilities — are just as important as government structure. Together with our transportation systems, they make up our infrastructure. Consciously or not, we deal with each part of this web everyday, and understanding how we must interact with it to address the year 2000 is crucial.

In the following discussion of the impact of the year 2000 problem on utilities, bear in mind that these systems are so interrelated that if one component fails, the whole system may well be shut down. If a safety device closes because it has a computer chip that cannot deal with a year 2000 date, it will not matter that the rest of the system is working perfectly: the end result will be no service.

The classic example of this is the great blackout of 1965, which began with the tripping of a single transmission line at a generating station, and in which the entire Eastern Seaboard lost power for 12 to 24 hours as a result. A similar instance in Quebec left 9 million people without power for 9 hours. Four million people in five western states and two Canadian provinces were affected by a similar problem in 1996. And these were because of problems that could be quickly identified and rapidly fixed.

Personally, I believe that in most of North America, these systems will continue to function at reasonable efficiency. But I would not bet on all of the systems in all of the rest of the world. And when you are talking about such basic human needs as power, heating, water, and communications, the implications of any one of these shutting down for more than a few hours can be scary indeed.

a. POWER UTILITIES

The challenge involved in solving the year 2000 problem for the power grids is enormous and fundamental to the operations of almost everything else. In general, the three major areas of concern are generating of power, distributing it, and tracking its usage for billing.

Electrical power can be generated in many different ways. It may come from hydro-electric generators, nuclear reactors, solar panels, coal or gas, or tidal generators. Each one of these systems uses electronic and computer operations that may be vulnerable to the year 2000 problem. If these fail to operate correctly, there won't be any electricity created in the first place. But even if it is produced, it still has to be distributed through an equally sophisticated system of power stations and transformers, safety mechanisms, and measuring meters. If any one of these fails to pass the Y2K test, the electricity may not reach our doors.

In some parts of North America, the supply of power is less than assured, and people living in these states or provinces have become used to brownouts or blackouts on a regular basis. Ironically, they may be better prepared for longer term failures than those of us who live in major cities. (And I truly believe that you should *expect* such occurrences and plan for them.)

First, make sure that your systems are adequately protected. Computers are notorious for disliking power problems, and a blackout can mean lost information, corrupted data, and applications that refuse to run. You need to become diligent about backing up information, installing surge protectors to deal with fluctuations in power, and installing uninterruptible power supplies (UPSs) to allow you to shut down systems in an orderly fashion rather than letting them crash. (A UPS is a device that detects a brownout or a blackout and gives you time, usually two to five minutes, in which to close down your computer systems in an orderly manner, even if the rest of the power has gone entirely.)

Second, you may want to look at installing your own generators as a backup power supply, and in some cases even establishing entire backup facilities as a safety measure for your company's computer operations. This latter step is appropriate only for very large companies, but it does emphasize that your level of planning for this eventuality should match the importance of the continued operation of your computer systems to the continued operations of the company itself. It goes without saying that you should make sure that these backup systems are themselves year 2000 ready.

Natural gas also provides another power source for most of us — one that we take for granted. But many readers will remember the winters in the early 1980s when there was not enough gas flowing through the distribution system to be able to satisfy all the heating demands across the continent.

I recently had to have a chip replaced in my hot water heater. The "broken" chip wouldn't allow the gas to flow because it couldn't detect the correct operation of another part of the heater. In fact, the rest of the heater was working perfectly, but the chip didn't know that. Until it could be replaced, I had no hot water.

If any part of the gas distribution system shuts down because of the failure of a microchip that cannot deal with a date in the next century, we may face a situation where we are unable to heat our homes and offices. And this of course is most likely to occur on January 1, 2000 — right in the middle of the winter.

Finally, even if power can be produced and distributed, the utility companies will still be in trouble if they cannot track the usage and bill it properly. We might be initially pleased at the prospect of a couple of months with no utility expenses, but not if that meant a subsequent inability for that company to deliver any power at all.

b. WATER

In chapter 7, I outlined the problems that would be caused by a failure in our water and waste management system. If any part of the grid fails, a basic commodity that we take for granted may not arrive out of our taps in the morning of January 1, 2000.

c. TELECOMMUNICATIONS

Telecommunication is the essential glue that transfers instructions from one person to another, one computer to another, and one business to another. What use is a hydro-electric dam if it doesn't know where to send its power? How can a transportation system move goods if it cannot receive messages to tell it where the goods are? To accomplish all of these information exchanges, we rely on electronic communication.

1. The all-pervasive grid

Telephones, fax machines, teletypes, cell phones, pagers, dispatch systems, satellite tracking services....the list is endless. And it is not merely the channel that we use that is important, but that channel's ability to transmit large volumes at high speed.

Imagine that your business had to return to relying solely on the postal service for your communication needs. That organization, too, is vulnerable to year 2000 problems, but the core element of its business, hard copy communication, may be safer and more reliable than an electronic transmission. Nevertheless, could you do the same volume of business if you received no faxes and limited phone calls? Even if your customers all used the mail, are you physically able to deal with opening envelopes, keying in all the data, making copies to send to all appropriate departments, and so on? No to mention the added time to mail out invoices and collect payment through a system that adds a minimum of a week to the process and more likely three or four.

The more sophisticated your business systems, the more you rely on fast and accurate communications, and the more vulnerable you are if any part your systems break down. Your smaller competitors, both here and abroad, that rely on these "primitive" (but ironically more reliable) communication systems have the edge in this situation.

2. The Internet

Businesses are increasingly conducting business communications via e-mail and the Internet, which means that they are also more vulnerable if those services fail.

But here's a bit of good news: the Internet may work when other communication systems fail. Initial evaluations suggest that it is free from any major risk from the year 2000 bug. But consider two factors. If any part of the system fails (your phone line, your Internet service provider, your Web page host, a section of the power system, your recipient's computer), your message will still fail to get through. And if you think the Internet is slow now, what happens if it suddenly becomes the only reliable worldwide communication system that still operates?

3. The telephone PBX system

The telephone is an indispensable item in both home and office. Whether we have a single line at home or a sophisticated telephone system in our office, we may again be dealing with problem microchips.

> "Virtually every enterprise is going to be impacted in some way," says Steve McElderry, the Santa Clara, California-based senior manager of call-center applications for Nortel Enterprise Networks in Richardson, Texas. The reason: "Practically every function on a private branch exchange phone system is ultimately controlled by the date," confirms Bart Stanco, an analyst with Gartner Group, an IT advisory firm in Stamford, Connecticut.

First you have to have a system that works in the first place, and if there is one errant microchip in your PBX system, your entire phone network may not work. Even if you have a two-person office with three or four phones, you may not be able to communicate with each other or with the outside world. And for more sophisticated enterprises, everything from transferring calls to voice mail, long distance charges to time and date stamping, may be lost.

Do you use a toll-free service of any kind, particularly one where you use an outside service to handle enquiries or take orders? If they aren't year 2000 compliant, such call centers could route customer service calls to the wrong destination, feed inaccurate data to other systems — or crash completely.

As much as 25% of installed call-center equipment may need to be replaced to handle year 2000, according to Dataquest, Inc. "People upgrade as little as possible," says Bruce Calhoon, president of Call Center Enterprises, a consulting firm in Cary, North Carolina." Call-center managers tend to be risk-averse," he says. "If their technology works, they don't upgrade it until they have to." If you lose this element of support or orders, what will that do for your business?

d. TRANSPORTATION SYSTEMS

Transportation and the government's involvement is discussed in the previous chapter. However, there are many elements of the system that are the responsibility of the private sector.

1. Fuel

The transportation systems of the industrialized world run on oil and its derivatives, primarily gasoline and diesel. Our ability to move large quantities of goods and people relies to an enormous extent on the availability of this raw material.

If you can remember the oil crisis of the 1970s, large numbers of workers could not function because they could not get gasoline for their vehicles. In that situation, of course, the problem was getting the oil to North America. Once an oil tanker reached a harbor, there was an established system in place to make sure that the oil could then be processed and reach its final destination efficiently and rapidly.

The difficulty with the year 2000 problem when applied to the distribution of gasoline is that, once again, you are dealing with a very complicated system with thousands of parts — from the oil tanker relying on a satellite positioning system to plot its course to the reliability of the gas station pumps and meters. And the problem extends to the whole system, not just the part outside North America. If any one of those parts breaks down, the gasoline may not reach your gas tank.

If you thought you were at risk of losing electrical power because the system is under the control of a single company, you must realize that the chances of the gasoline system working perfectly through dozens of intercompany transactions is even less likely. In fact, we already know that certain elements will crash, specifically the Geostationary Positioning System (GPS) satellite system. This is due to fail on August 21, 1999. The system will have its date reset to read January 7, 1980, to prevent this crash.

The latter is not a year 2000 problem, although it may add to the Y2K mess. But it again comes from the malfunction of a programming chip whose life was not expected to last for 20 years and be connected with dozens of other non-military systems.

2. Schedules

Let us assume that all the vehicles on road, rail, and sea can get enough fuel to power their operations. Does this solve the overall operation of the global transportation system? Probably not. With an ever-increasing amount of traffic of all kinds, we rely more and more on sophisticated traffic control and scheduling systems. And these are more date-dependent than almost any other series of systems we use on a daily basis.

Consider the scheduling systems we encounter. In large cities, mass transit moves a large number of people, whether by commuter train, subway, bus, or streetcar. People rely on a huge network of interlocking schedules.

Train stations and bus depots are complicated enough, but an airport is at another level entirely. Besides the schedules for flights and passengers, there are a whole series of timetables for preparing aircraft for fueling, cleaning, mechanical servicing, and safety checks, quite apart from moving goods and luggage, security checks, delivery of flight personnel, and so on.

e. WHAT CAN I DO?

Most utility companies are aware of the year 2000 problem and have started converting their systems in order to be ready. Within each organization, there are many computer and other electronic systems that must be tested and changed. Some of these relate to safety issues, some to distribution of products, and others to billing and other financial aspects of the utility. For all of these utilities, if one part of the system breaks down, it is likely that this will mean the entire system becomes unworkable, even if just for a short period.

There is only a limited amount that we as businesses or as individuals can do if these systems fail for a long period. We can prepare ourselves for some days when there is limited power, heat, or telecommunications, but few of us are self-sufficient enough to be able to survive for a long time without these services. Most businesses are so dependent on computers that without their own electrical generators all of their systems will be totally unable to operate.

As part of your year 2000 preparations, then, you must work on a contingency plan and investigate how you may be able to operate your business with manual systems, especially to cover temporary or permanent communication glitches. (See chapter 10, which covers the year 2000 plan in detail.) It is unlikely that you will be able to operate all aspects of your business without working utilities. Nevertheless, core operations may well be able to continue, and if you have prepared for such an eventuality today, you may have a major advantage over your competition.

But perhaps, most importantly, make sure that everyone you know is aware of the problem and working toward solving it. Phone your hydro and gas companies, talk to your local mass transit authority, contact your local courier company, and raise the issue with your regular airline. Yes you may be initially fobbed off with a trite reply, but the more people who raise the issue the more likely it is to be addressed and solved. The alternative is far less attractive.

9
DOLLARS AND SENSE: FINANCIAL ORGANIZATIONS AND THE YEAR 2000

Ever since civilization moved from the barter system, money has become the common denominator that connects all segments of society throughout the world. Whether we pay someone's salary, purchase goods or materials, or transfer funds — we expect all of these transactions to take place smoothly, easily and, more and more often, *electronically*.

The transfer of money between different parties depends on our financial institutions — banks, insurance companies, trust companies, and brokerage houses. A large number of smaller institutions provide specialized financial services to all these institutions.

In general, financial institutions became aware of the year 2000 problem early on. Because they frequently deal with investments that have a life of more than five years (such as mortgages, life insurance, guaranteed investment certificates, and savings bonds), between 1990 and 1993 many of them found that their systems could not deal with the calculations required to set up many financial transactions. As a group, they are well advanced in their year 2000 planning.

The problem is that financial institutions are more interconnected than perhaps any other industry. This means that unless *everything* works perfectly on January 1, 2000, the domino effect of one bank's or even one system's failure can have enormous consequences.

a. BANKS

Banks interconnect with *everyone:* hundreds of countries, millions of businesses, hundreds of millions of computers. Overall, the clearinghouse for interbank payment systems coordinates daily bank-to-bank transactions worth nearly $2 trillion. Their systems are more complicated than any other institution's, with the possible exception of government, and probably the most vulnerable to problems in other systems.

Most companies have daily dealings with their bank and would be placed at extreme risk if they did not have immediate access to it. From simple activities like depositing checks to the fundamental issue of being able to clear payroll, a company needs its bank to be instantly visible. In many cases, delays of even a few days may put a company at risk, especially those trading in large volumes at small margins.

There are at least three types of failures a bank could experience because of year 2000:

(a) Failure of deposit and withdrawal systems

(b) Failure of reporting systems

(c) Failure of service systems

As well, banks could be faced with huge cash withdrawals as we near January 1, 2000.

1. Failure of deposit and withdrawal systems

When a check is presented at a bank, the bank depends on its record-keeping facilities to tell it whether it can pay the amount. Systems may look for the current balance, any overdrafts, a recent deposit that still needs time to clear, signature authorities, and other items, and it does all this while you are standing at the teller waiting to get your money. If any one of these processes fails, the bank may not be able to tell whether it can honor the check or not.

If you use an automated teller machine (ATM), different information may be searched for (e.g., PIN numbers, daily limit on withdrawals), and it, too, needs a functioning communications network that connects to a central information depository on a 24-hour basis. If this equipment fails, it means a return to waiting for an available teller. Even if a teller has the information to authorize the financial transaction, the number of tellers has been greatly reduced in the past few years with the introduction of electronic banking. So not only are there fewer people to satisfy the demand for face-to-face banking, the demand itself will increase by two to three times (at least) because there could be no other options for dealing with your bank if the systems fail.

2. Failure of reporting systems

Once a month, your bank sends you your bank statement showing your opening balance (on a specific date), increases from deposits (organized by date), reductions due to check payments and other charges (also organized by date), and a closing balance (dated).

If a problem occurs in just one of these elements, it will throw off the entire statement. As a consumer, you may like it having your mortgage money stay in your account for an extra month or two, but you won't appreciate it when your credit rating suddenly collapses because of non-payment of that same item. Nor will you like it when the system's failure means that your paycheck doesn't get transferred from another bank to your account.

If the system fails in this way, you may well have enough information in your own financial systems to identify what is missing and make the necessary adjustments and corrections. But imagine what happens if bank systems start *miscalculating*.

Suppose, for example, that on February 3, 2000, you get your bank statement for January 2000. Everything looks fine except for the interest charge on your outstanding balance. The computer says that the overdraft of $2,000 that existed on December 31, 1999, has accrued an interest cost of $4,071,631.96 (at 8% interest for 99 years). Your bookkeeper estimates the correct amount and enters it in the system and adjusts your books, and of course you complain to the bank, along with 400,000 other customers. But in the meantime your account is frozen because you are wildly overdrawn, and the next month's statement arrives with another charge for February of $325,890.56!

3. Failure of service systems

Of course, a big part of a bank's business is lending money, particularly business loans and mortgages. That lending also extends to lines of credit and credit cards. From a business point of view, credit card authorization services may also be a key part of your company sales and operations.

Most businesses cannot operate at their present level without a line of credit, and if it were withdrawn, many would not be able to operate at all. Loan levels could be reduced for a variety of reasons ranging from failure of the company's accounting system, general retrenchment on the part of the bank, failure in the bank's own systems for tracking loans, and miscalculations of bank balances. Whatever the cause, the loss of operating lines of credit could stimulate a dramatic economic slowdown, as well as an increase in business closures and bankruptcies.

Further, the security for these loans could be at risk. Typically a loan will be secured by assets, such as real estate or shares. If there is any drastic change in the value of this security, there may be insufficient security to hold the loan at its present level. On the other hand, there will probably not be enough liquidity in the system to give the borrower enough cash to pay down all or part of the loan.

4. Cash withdrawals

Some people have speculated that there may be a large amount of cash withdrawn from the banking system in the last few months of 1999. This may occur because of general economic fears, but will more probably be related to people's fears that they will not be able to use ATM machines, credit and debit cards, or even checks in the early part of the year 2000.

The dollar figure could be huge. Personal needs aside, the amount of cash needed if a lot of companies decided to withdraw two months' wages in cash would amount to billions of dollars. There simply may not be enough cash in the financial system.

This scenario could well cause a run on one or more banks if people start to believe that one particular bank is insolvent. Under current legislation, a bank is required to hold only a certain amount of its funds in *current* assets. When a bank issues a mortgage, it lends money on a long-term basis, and it cannot suddenly collapse that mortgage to free up cash for a short-term need. So even a bank with an enormous amount of long-term assets could face a severe financial crunch if it needed a large amount of cash on a short-term basis.

5. Bank failures

None of the discussion so far has considered the question of what happens if the bank itself fails, which could happen for several reasons, including:

(a) failed systems,

(b) non-compliant systems,

(c) lack of liquidity because of withdrawals of cash from one bank, and

(d) lack of confidence in the banking system itself.

Don't count on the deposit insurance that exists in both Canada and the United States to protect you from such failures. The insurance program puts aside a very small percentage of all deposits in the expectation that this amount will be enough should there be a collapse of a *few* banks. It was not designed to deal with the large-scale collapse of many banks.

The other problem is that even if the system works, the time factor in getting back your insured deposit may be months or even years. After all, you may be lining up with hundreds of thousands or even millions of people. The process of identifying the amounts covered (from screwed-up records), getting the necessary releases, and issuing the checks is likely to take a very long time.

6. The state of readiness

In Canada, there are a limited number of large banks. All of these organizations are well aware of the year 2000 problem, and are well advanced in their contingency plans. This doesn't mean that they are less susceptible to problems related to the systems with which they connect, but it does mean that the overall system is a lot stronger than in the United States. The banks have even started discussion among themselves about how they might communicate with each other if there is a major failure of telecommunication systems.

In the United States, the situation is not as developed. There are a far greater number of banks and most of them operate regionally rather than nationally. Many of the large national ones are well advanced, but this is not the case with many of the state banks. Some may be able to react faster because the size of the systems with which they have to deal is smaller. On the other hand, many of them remain unaware of the problem or are unprepared to devote the necessary resources to fixing it. Many rely on third parties to run their computer systems and that, of course, includes correcting any year 2000 errors in their code.

b. INSURANCE COMPANIES

Insurance companies may be the quiet giants of financial institutions, if only because the dealings we have with them on a business basis rarely expose the billions of dollars they have in assets. They, too, are long-time computer users, and they, too, are faced with upgrading their old legacy systems to be compliant with the date schemes of the new century.

A business will usually deal directly with an insurance company on three fronts:

(a) Equipment and property insurance

(b) Benefit plans for its principals and employees

(c) Liability coverage related to loss of business, bonding, directors' liabilities, etc.

The year 2000 bug will affect all three of these areas. While breakdowns in equipment are unlikely to be covered by insurance plans, there may be more claims as a result of non-functional alarm systems, particularly if there is significant loss due to a robbery or fire. Benefit plans may not be directly affected, but many companies will have problems with their overall payroll systems. There are likely to be slowdowns in processing claims due to communication problems. This will affect claim verifications and confirmations, as well as calculations for amounts that include deductibles and upper limits, etc.

Many businesses have two insurance policies to take care of liability. One of them provides compensation should the business be shut down for a period for reasons beyond their control. The other protects their directors and officers in case of lawsuits against them from shareholders, employees, or other creditors of the company.

1. Business interruption insurance

Business interruption insurance is usually invoked when the company undergoes a catastrophic event of some kind. Typically, this might include a flood or a fire. The importance of this type of insurance was demonstrated during the recent flooding in the Red River Valley in North Dakota and Manitoba in 1997. Many businesses were closed because of the floods and some went out of business. Many failed because they did not have the resources to sustain a prolonged period of forced inactivity. With no cash flow from customers, they had no reserves to allow them to survive for an extra two or three months. On top of this, many lost all of their business information and had no backups from which they could restore their data or their systems.

Like the devastating flood of 1997, the year 2000 crisis may force many companies to cease operations for a time. But in theory, it is an avoidable problem, and insurance companies are moving to change their policies to avoid liability should a business decide to claim under their business interruption coverage. You can argue whether or not this is fair, but the reality is you may see additional clauses inserted into your standard insurance renewals in 1997 and 1998, and certainly by 1999.

2. Directors' liability insurance

Directors are generally not personally liable for a company's debts, except for some responsibility for back wages and remittances to the government for salary withholdings. They *may*, however, be considered liable if through a lack of prudence or a failure to take their responsibilities seriously they failed in their fiscal responsibility to the shareholders of the company. There have been an increasing number of shareholder actions in the past two decades pursuing this last point, and a corresponding reluctance by individuals to act as company directors.

The best way to protect directors from that liability has been to have insurance coverage. But that coverage is to protect against events that they could not reasonably predict. As discussed earlier in this book, the year 2000 problem is definitely foreseeable, so it is not entirely unreasonable that insurance companies are moving to eliminate the possibility for directors to be able to claim that the collapse of a business from year 2000–related problems should be covered by their director's insurance.

3. Historical data

Insurance companies rely heavily on historical data. They need it to establish the actuarial trends that help them develop new products and refine old ones. Whether they choose to convert or abandon some of that information will depend on the individual companies, but some of the information may not be available to even small firms following the start of the new millennium.

And miscalculations may also occur. In one case, an insurance company promised that 15 years after an initial investment of $10,000, a policy holder would receive a return of $50,000. Hundreds of these policies were sold before an individual with some common sense investigated the calculation and discovered that the computer had calculated the growth based on an overall life span of 135 years.

Not only does this example show the financial risks that a large institution may incur as a result of the year 2000 problem, but it also clearly indicates how much we rely on computers. No one during the policy's initial marketing questioned the financial results as calculated by the insurance company's own internal systems.

c. STOCK MARKETS AND BROKERAGE HOUSES

The business world will be affected by the year 2000 action on the stock market in two ways: its traditional role as an arbiter of all kinds of financial transactions will be at risk, along with the integrity of its own performance.

1. Raising capital

Stock exchanges were originally established to allow companies to raise capital. This could be done through the selling of financial instruments, typically common or preferred shares, but also bonds and debentures. Over the years as free market economies developed, they also have played an important role in their interaction with government borrowing, interest rates, and currency exchange rates. Brokerage houses are also key in establishing investor confidence in shares being traded on the stock exchanges of the world.

To accomplish all of their transactions, stock exchanges, like the banks, have established enormous and highly complex electronic systems to help them perform the billions of transfers they make between millions of individuals and institutions each year. These systems are now at risk.

Smith Barney, a very large brokerage firm in the United States, recently demonstrated the risks of introducing an error into large, complicated systems. As part of its solution to the year 2000 problem, it expanded its date field from six digits (YYMMDD) to eight (YYYYMMDD). To do this, they added 19,000,000 to each field; for example, 19,000,000 plus 970515 (May 15, 1997) creates the new date 19970515.

But instead of adding the figure to the date field, they added it to the outstanding balance field! With over 500,000 accounts, they increased the net worth of their clients by almost $10 trillion! Luckily, they caught their error almost immediately. And it was lucky that even 1,000 clients did not have the opportunity to withdraw their instant millions, as this would have cost the firm its life.

Another important internal system may also face a challenge in the early part of the new millennium. Most international jurisdictions require that the transactions stockbrokers undertake on behalf of a client be settled within three trading days. This is to discourage people from trading with money that they don't have in the hope that their profits will pay the bill before they themselves have to. But it is easy to imagine that with a computer failure, a broker may be unable to satisfy this rule, causing immense problems for the buyer, the seller, and the broker caught in between.

2. **Stock market performance**

At the time of writing, the stock exchange was on an extremely hot streak. The Dow Jones was hitting new records, and some predictions have it growing another 10% to 20%. It has undergone a couple of minor corrections, but the end of the current bull session is still not in sight. Public confidence has rarely been higher.

The year 2000 crisis could change that, both in the short term and in the long term. First, although the costs of the year 2000 are only just starting to show up on financial statements, the overall costs will be significant. In many cases that means significant reductions in earnings per share.

All of these amounts are significant, and range from 2% to 10% of present earnings. Since company valuations are based on a price/earnings ratio (a multiple representing the price of the share divided by its earnings per share), earnings have a direct effect of the valuation on the market. So if a company's profits are going to drop by 2% to 10% over the next 6 to 12 months, there is a strong argument to be made that the value of the market as a whole should also decrease by that amount.

This reduction will have a domino effect. Some investment funds are taking steps to protect their investors from the vagaries of companies that won't consider year 2000 issues. Scottish Widows Insurance Group is refusing to invest in companies that fail to update their computer systems to cope with the expected millennium computer crisis. Already the insurer has sold shares worth £30 million in two American companies because these companies did not satisfy its tough criteria. It says the issue has become a key consideration in its investment strategy. Alan Denholm, the head of Scottish Widows' American desk, said in the *Sunday Times* (March 16, 1997): "A company's ability to handle the problem could have a serious bearing on its performance. We are asking all our existing and potential clients if they appreciate what impact the millennium might have on their company, and if they have made provision for it."

In the longer term, over the next two years the probability is that year 2000 news will only serve to reduce market confidence. There will be increasing news about the costs that it will carry. Then there will be more information about industries and companies that are failing to maintain their timetables. At home, the failure of some government departments will become more public and overseas investors will have additional concerns about foreign governments that are not doing enough. Finally you must add in the public's lack of optimism about the economy as the lessons of the year 2000 experts start to be heard, and increased litigation from companies frightened about their risk exposure.

I recognize that there are many other factors that affect the price of shares, the volatility of stock prices, and the movement of the markets. But there is no question that as the costs of year 2000 start to be seen on the bottom-line, it will have a dampening effect on share prices. And that will be further exacerbated when the Securities Commissions and professional accountants associations finally decide on the rules for required disclosure of year 2000 risk — for every publicly traded company around the world.

I hope I'm wrong. There may be a more gradual slowdown in the economy. Perhaps the government will start to become more concerned in the short term so that we will collectively start moving faster to address the complex issues that this problem presents for our political and economic agendas. I am going to be cautious with such hopes. In your business planning, I think you should be too.

3. Opportunities

Whenever there is volatility in the markets, there is the opportunity to make money. Bearish investors by definition make their investments on the basis that a *decrease* of prices is coming, not an increase. In chapter 17 there is a somewhat more complete discussion of the investment opportunities related to the year 2000 crisis, but this book is not in any way trying to provide you with specific investment advice. Should you require this kind of information, an experienced professional is the best person to advise you.

However, as a small business owner, you must do what you can to protect your business from the impact of the probable challenges that will be faced by these financial services, particularly if it will affect your own ability to properly run your company operations.

PART III

YOUR YEAR 2000 PLAN

10
GROUND RULES FOR THE YEAR 2000 PLAN

You understand what the problem is and how it may affect you. What do you do now to organize yourself, protect your business, and make sure that all of your operations are year 2000 compliant?

There is no silver bullet, no miracle cure that will solve this problem in all your hardware and software. There is a methodology that you can follow — a set of steps that apply to all businesses. Following them will ensure that you have considered all the possible ramifications of the year 2000 bug on your operations and corrected them to the greatest extent possible.

Not all businesses will place the same emphasis on the same components of the process. For example, a company with 100 overseas suppliers will have a different communication plan than one that deals with half a dozen North American suppliers. The size of your firm, too, will obviously make a difference. However, all companies should consider all of the areas for discussion laid out below.

In this section of the book, chapters 10 to 16, I lay out the plan's basic elements. This chapter provides the overview that top management will need; subsequent chapters cover each area in detail, from safeguarding inventory to establishing communications.

a. RULE #1: ENSURE TOP-DOWN SUPPORT

The first step you must take is to *make absolutely, positively sure* that the senior management of your company understands the problem, understands what it will take to fix it, and is completely committed to the fact that it is a problem that must be fixed. If you are a company owner, I hope I have provided you with enough information so that this will not be an issue. If, however, you are a manager in a larger enterprise, you are likely to have to sell the issue to get that universal support.

Providing books and reference materials on the subject is a good way to introduce the subject to your executive team. The Internet is also a good source of information. Finally, year 2000 consulting companies are more than pleased to have the opportunity to brief management about the issues. You may well find a strong outside supporter in your company's auditors. See Appendix 2 for a list of information resources.

You mustn't underestimate the difficulty of bringing the executive team on line, and of ensuring that everyone else in the company becomes part of the solution. There are still business leaders of large corporations with years of street smarts who fail to recognize the enormity of the problem, or who believe that an instant solution will be found.

b. RULE #2: FORM YOUR MANAGEMENT COMMITTEE

Once you have obtained your senior executive's endorsement, you should immediately move to strike a coordinating committee. There are some obvious managers, or at least departments, who should participate, including accounting and information technology personnel. But to make sure that you get company-wide activity on the actions required, you should also include staff from sales and marketing, production (if applicable), personnel, and purchasing.

I also strongly recommend that at least the first meeting of this committee should be attended by the managers from each department. You may have to spend one or two hours convincing them of the size of the problem, just as you may have had to do with the senior executives. It is, however, time well spent. While they themselves may not have the time to participate on the committee, they need to understand the seriousness of the problem.

c. RULE #3: APPOINT A PROJECT LEADER

One of the first steps that the committee should undertake is to appoint a single project leader. This person should act as the single coordinator of all information related to the year 2000. Ideally, this person will also have the authority to speak directly to the president or owner of the company about the issue.

No matter how unified the committee appears to be, year 2000 involves tradeoffs between present and future projects as well as between departments. It is natural that you will run into disagreements about what needs to be done and probably whose budgets will be affected. If the year 2000 project manager encounters a problem that cannot be resolved easily, either within a particular department or by the coordinating committee, he or she will need a decision quickly, and one that sticks. You and your company cannot afford the year 2000 problem to be derailed or sidelined by interdepartmental wrangling or office politics.

Depending on the size of the company and the size of its year 2000 problem, the project manager may spend all or part of his or her time on this issue. But don't just add the task of project manager to someone else's current responsibilities. This will almost certainly lead to its priority being downgraded and the project falling behind.

If the present staff are already working flat out, the committee may wish to recommend that someone new be hired. This might be on a full-time or a part-time basis, or it may be a contract position. Another alternative may be to hire an outside individual (or firm) who would come in one day a week or one day a month (or whatever timetable makes sense), to manage the company's project.

There are advantages and disadvantages in all of these approaches, and all of them carry different amounts of dollar costs. The choice made will reflect the company's situation and may have to be a compromise based on the realities of staff and other resources. The coordination committee should, however, do its utmost to ensure that the person chosen to do the job has both the abilities and the mandate to carry out what needs to be done efficiently and effectively. (See chapter 11 for a discussion on hiring choices.)

d. RULE #4: UNDERSTAND THE SPECIAL NATURE OF THE PROJECT

1. Scope of the plan

Fixing the year 2000 problem is unlike most other projects that your business has undertaken. It is a project that is almost overwhelming in size, it changes frequently in scope and emphasis, it has rigid deadlines, and it may have continually escalating costs. If management does not understand this, it is likely that any personnel asked to become involved will see it as an invitation to becoming a scapegoat for a project that, by its nature, is unlikely to conform to its original budget and timetable.

There is a saying in business: "Fast, good, and cheap; pick two out of three." In other words, you can't have all three; most projects require tradeoffs.

The year 2000 leaves you with limited options. In this case, the project must be good: 99% accuracy may not be enough. It is also a project that must be done to a very specific deadline: December 31, 1999. This means that fast is an absolute requirement, and again a standard that cannot be bent or extended. Given that these two factors are relatively incapable of compromise, you can easily see the only variable left. And from watching the information and news on this subject, prices appear to be rising rapidly.

2. Lack of choice

Usually a business has a number of projects underway and a number of other initiatives planned. Typically, an initiative will turn into a project if it can show that its pay-back is greater than its costs. In other words, it must be demonstrated that it can help increase revenue or decrease expenses, that the company has the resources needed to complete the project, and, on an overall basis, that its collective benefits are more than other competing proposals.

But this is not the case with the year 2000 project. Although there may be some opportunities to improve company operations, the main thrust of the plan may well be to spend a considerable amount of time and effort to bring to the company systems at almost exactly the same level of operation being attained today. It is a project that demands that sufficient resources be made available, regardless of whether they can be drawn from within the company's supplies at present, and regardless of whether the money is in the bank. It is an initiative whose priority moves to the top of the list immediately and without discussion.

3. Time frames

> In a 1996 survey which analyzed over 7,000 information systems projects, the consulting company Capers Jones found that the probability of late projects ranged from 22% in the best-run information system shops to 85% in the worst-run establishments. The probability that the project would be canceled ranged from 1% to 40%. In the case of the year 2000, cancelation is not an option. So translating these figures, there is almost a guaranteed one-in-four chance that the project will not be completed according to the original time frame.

The establishment of a timetable and an accurate critical path with enough flexibility is very important to the whole project. The challenge is that such a schedule cannot be written in stone, because more tasks, more complications, and more delays will keep arriving on the project coordinator's doorstep.

Some studies have been done to estimate the percentage of time of the whole project that must be spent on each stage. While these estimates relate to larger enterprises where the correction of internal code and the testing of those corrections will take up much more time than for most small- and medium-sized enterprises, they are nevertheless illuminating. Table #2 displays the figures.

This schedule shows that the vast majority of the time will not be spent in identifying systems to be corrected or even in establishing the overall scope of the project, although both of these activities may represent several weeks of work for a medium-sized business. Most of the work will come in the

TABLE #2
PERCENTAGE OF TIME OF WHOLE PROJECT SPENT ON INDIVIDUAL SEGMENTS

Awareness	1%
Taking inventory	1%
Project scoping	4%
Examination, analysis, and solutions design	20%
Modification	20%
Unit test	25%
Systems test	15%
Integration/User acceptance	5%
Implementation, disaster recovery, documentation	9%

Adapted from information supplied by the Gartner Group "INSPECT Process Analysis."

first phase, where you are fixing the problems, whether through repair or replacement. The second phase will involve testing those fixes in all of the systems to make sure they function correctly.

4. Cost influences

Most business projects have an allocated budget at the time of their approval. The project manager is traditionally expected to confine expenditures to that budget, and the ability to remain on track financially is often the measure of a manager's performance.

Your year 2000 budget will have to be considered differently. First, you can expect that the scope of the project as originally conceived will expand. You may find you have more software than you expected. You may find that replacing a system, while more expensive, is in fact the more effective business decision. You will almost certainly find that communicating with your suppliers and customers takes up more time and dollars than you anticipate. You will probably underestimate your labor costs, because much of the work may be done at overtime rates rather than regular hourly rates.

Another problem is estimating the costs to come from any consultants you engage. You can afford to spend a small amount of time shopping around, but the longer you shop, the more chance that prices will go up. This is just the reverse of your usual efforts to find the best price.

> In Canada, one leading consulting firm has quoted CDN $750 per day in 1997, $1,000 per day in 1998, and $1,250 per day in 1999 for year 2000 consulting services. In the United States, rates of US $1,000 and $1,500 are already being quoted.

The Texas state government recently added a provision in its Appropriations Act giving state agencies and universities the authority to grant bonuses of up to $5,000 per year to year 2000 workers. This sounds good — until your read about the strings attached:

(a) The employee must have been employed for the past three years and be defined as "critical."

(b) The bonus can be no more than $5,000 in fiscal year 1998 or 1999.

(c) Any increases must be derived from existing agency budgets.

(d) The employee must sign an employment contract agreeing to work through May 31, 2000.

In reality, existing budgets are insufficient and many IT workers don't remain with one organization for two years, let alone three. The daily rates that are being offered in private industry would allow them to recoup the annual bonus in under a week. If these workers understand the year 2000 issue, they will refuse to sign such a restrictive employment contract.

So while on the one hand, the Texas state government obviously understands some of the year 2000 issues by being prepared to offer the bonus in the first place, the restrictions it is trying to impose shows that it does not understand what is happening in the outside marketplace.

The other challenge that will arise is that as other countries become aware of the problem, they will come searching for experts in the countries that are farthest ahead — Canada and the United States. So even if we are farther ahead right now, we may also face more setbacks and loss of staff than other countries that are presently behind us in making preparations. You should expect that your best employees will be approached by other firms.

5. Shortage of resources

If you are a company of sufficient size to have permanent information technology people on staff, you are probably already aware how difficult it is to find the right person and how expensive it will be to hire. This situation is worse with year 2000, because no one has any experience in solving it; in almost every case, the person being hired has never done the job he or she is being hired to do.

In smaller enterprises, it may not be as important that the project coordinator have a high level of technical skill; the best individual may well be one who has a broad understanding of a wide range of business departments and operations. After all, this person has to be able to deal with all of your departments, not just focus on accounting or IT. In other words, you are looking for a generalist, and in this day and age when specialization has been seen to be the only approach to career advancement, this kind of person is very hard to find.

The bad news is that this situation is likely only to get worse. Capers Jones is the chairman of Software Productivity Research, a highly respected consulting firm based in Burlington, MA. His paper "The Global Economic Impact of the Year 2000 Software Problem" is considered one of the definitive texts on the issue. He estimates there are approximately two million IT professionals in the world. He also estimates that there are more than 32 million applications to fix, and that does not include spreadsheets, an application that millions of companies use for evaluation and reporting purposes. This means that each professional must fix 16 or more applications, an unlikely schedule at best. So if it is hard to find an appropriately skilled person today, it may become even more difficult tomorrow as year 2000 awareness rises and supply shrinks further.

e. RULE #5: SET THE SCHEDULE

One of the biggest challenges that year 2000 brings to business is the enormous time commitment over and above the regular schedule. For some companies, a time commitment like this may be solved by the expenditure of dollars. In other words, if you don't have the time available yourself, you can purchase resources.

Smaller companies rarely have any amount of extra cash, and they frequently have no additional time to invest in a new problem. One of your primary jobs will be to establish the schedule you need to follow and determine the external timetables you must consider. This will help you decide if you have a choice between investing in time and dollars.

1. **Set your deadlines**

The first date to establish is when you must have all the replacement work and conversions completed. This date may not be January 1, 2000. Unfortunately, in many cases that is the latest possible deadline. There may be a number of factors that move this date forward and reduce the amount of available time with which you have to work.

First, consider your financial year end. In almost every case, particularly as it relates to changes in the accounting system, this will be the best possible time to change systems, whether repairing or replacing them.

Second, other companies with which you have to work may influence your deadline. You may be one of a number of subsidiaries in a large diversified corporation. You may have a number of business partners with whom you work closely, and with whom you would have to coordinate any schedules related to year 2000. You may also have to deal with seasonal or even annual cycles if these are part of your industry and can be predicted with some certainty.

Third, you must consider the overall state of your computers and any current projects. For example, are you already in the process of upgrading a number of your microcomputers as a general part of your business growth and change? In this case, it may make sense to complete your hardware upgrades before you tackle the year 2000 issue, and you should check to make sure that the year 2000 problem itself will not alter the parameters of other initiatives already begun.

Finally, you need to consider the purity of the data you already have in your computer system. If you have been operating for a number of years, you may find that some date fields in your database have been used to store information other than dates. In some systems, a valid date must be entered before an operator can go on to enter other details. Some companies have already found that a year entry of 99 was often made if the data entry operator did not know what year should apply. Other times, an entry of 9/9/99 was made as a trigger to indicate that another action needed to be checked and corrected. Many years later, these have all become valid dates!

You may have to complete work before these bits of rogue data affect your operations. If your year end is October 31, for example, any rogue data or "disinformation" buried in your system may make September 9, 1999, a time bomb. This means that your deadline for a complete new system is October 31, 1998. In order to factor in a year's lead time, you should have embarked on this project "yesterday"! Alternatively, you may have to allow for the additional amount of time it will take to go through your systems and clean out all of this material before you can then start on the changeover of any repair or replacement programs.

2. Determine how much time you have

You may think that you have the time between now and the deadline you have now set, which in the best of all possible worlds is until December 31, 1999. Once again, this is not realistic. From January 1, 1998, to December 31, 1999, there are 729 days, but taking into account weekends, public holidays, vacation time, and sick leave, you're left with about 430 working days.

Let us suppose that you operate a company with nine employees. It is likely that one-third of your employees cannot play a major role in the project, and another third are already too busy to be able to devote much time to it. If the remaining third are working at 95% capacity and can absorb another 5% workload, you may be able to get 21 days from each of them or 60 to 70 days in total over a two-year period!

If the work is carefully planned and scheduled, if you bring in extra help as needed, and if you don't fall behind on your deadlines, this may be enough to do what needs to be done. But it is yet another call to start immediately. If you estimate that the project will take that 60 days and halfway through 1999 you realize it will take another 30, you will suddenly be placing a huge amount of pressure on your staff, your time, and your pocketbook.

3. Run parallel systems and test

You should plan on doing a parallel systems run to confirm that the old and new systems produce identical results. At the very least, you should do extensive testing between both sets of programs to make absolutely sure that this is the case.

Typically, in changing over accounting systems, the parallel run will be two or three months. Allow for an additional month after this test to correct any mistakes that have been found. Keep in mind, however, that accounting year ends are often established in the slowest time of year for the company's operations and doing a parallel run to test the data at that time may not provide the best validation of the new system.

4. Set those deadlines — again!

Having considered all the factors discussed above, you can confirm the date when the project must be completed. Now what you have to do is look backwards from this date, add in all of the planning and execution stages, and you should be able to calculate when you need to start. In many cases you may find that your starting date has already passed; this is an alarm bell that should prompt you to apply more resources to your systems.

And don't forget to allow time for contingency plans. If electronic systems fail to operate, you need to determine the difference between critical and non-critical systems. If the computers fail, your product or service must still get out the door, even if all the paperwork is completed by hand. You need a contingency plan for the non-essential systems because you may not have the time and resources available to repair or replace them.

This process, too, will take time, time that you must work into your overall schedule. And if you do have to establish alternative processes for the systems that are crucial to your operations, recognize that it can take *a lot* of time.

f. RULE #6: START NOW!

While the size and scope of the steps described above may be discouraging, it sends a clarion call for major action. That activity is: START NOW!

If you start on the project right away, you will realize the following benefits:

- You are more likely to achieve your deadlines.
- You will have a better chance at finding and retaining qualified personnel.
- You will do a more thorough job.
- You will save money.
- You will achieve a major advantage over your competitors earlier on.
- You win an opportunity to gain more customers.
- You are more likely to win a leadership position within your industry and your community.
- You will extract the maximum amount of time to take advantage of the opportunities within this situation.

11
HOW TO HIRE THE RIGHT PERSON FOR THE JOB

So now you have your timetable. Do you staff it from inside or from outside?

a. USING INSIDE STAFF

Most small- and medium-sized enterprises run on personal computers, perhaps with a network, but without a lot of custom-written code. If this is your situation, then the person charged with overseeing the "fix" is probably not a programmer but rather a project manager and may be someone you already have on staff. After all, the best person will be someone who understands your business. Someone with strong technical and programming skills but with no understanding of your marketing or production department's concerns probably won't do.

Whether you plan to promote from within or you plan to hire someone new, a potential manager with the required experience and skills offers many potential advantages to your company. Prospective candidates should have the following capabilities:

- Be experienced enough to hold an intermediate to senior position with responsibility for reporting to the president or executive committee.
- Have or be capable of acquiring a comprehensive understanding of all company operations.
- Hold strong computer literacy skills.
- Have good communication skills.
- Be a strategic thinker.

If you define the job this way, it may make it easier to hire someone. After all, if you look for a person to fill the position of year 2000 project manager, there may be an inherent assumption by you and the employee that the job will end on January 1, 2000, or even earlier. This will not encourage long-term loyalty to your firm. As already pointed out, there may well be attractive opportunities dangled in front of anyone who can demonstrate year 2000 experience. Without a commitment to a long-term staffing position, you could suddenly find yourself with a major hole in your carefully constructed plan.

On the other hand, you could consider hiring a project or operations executive or perhaps a general manager whose first responsibility is to address the year 2000 problem but whose roll will expand after that is accomplished. In doing so, you may succeed in developing a plan that can make your overall company staffing a lot stronger.

Your choices as to how to staff this position obviously depend on your company. Where you are today, your present staff's expertise, and where you want the firm to be tomorrow will all play a role. Realize that the person you are considering could well be an important link in your overall chain of command, not just a programming hack who you will stick in a dark corner and then abandon when he or she has completed the contract.

It may be, too, that you can divide the tasks you need done between several people. This does *not* mean you can do away with the idea of a project manager; at the end of the day, you still need a single chief on this project. But you may find that some specific steps can be divided up among existing staff members. The following chart shows one type of plan:

TASK	DONE BY
Inventory of hardware and software	Management information system staff person
Evaluation of systems	Year 2000 committee
Financial impacts and budgets	Accounting department
Strategic implications	Executive committee
Communications plans	Sales and marketing department

Again I emphasize, *don't presume that the tasks associated with the year 2000 challenge can easily be fitted into a regular workload.* You should budget for the extra time costs; if you don't, you may lose overworked and undercompensated staff. The best people who will do the best job may already be working for you — if you can collectively figure out the optimum way to share the tasks involved.

b. HIRING OUTSIDE CONSULTANTS

The resources you need will depend on the size of the problem, which will often relate to the size of your company. Your knowledge of your systems and other internal resources also has a bearing on the problem's scope. If you know your systems well, have good staff, and the problem is relatively simple, you may want to hire a specific individual with expertise in a particular type of system. This allows you to stay on top of the problem and check the consultant's findings. If the consultant quits, it won't be a disaster because you'll have the resources to carry on from where he or she left off. But if the project is larger and your timetable more critical, you may choose to hire someone from a large firm that offers more depth of personnel; this way, you'll be able to continue to move forward even if the actual consultant changes.

1. Determining the tasks

First, define the tasks that you want the consultant or consulting firm to complete. Even if you want the consultant to undertake the entire project, it is still going to take a considerable time commitment from your staff, and there are certain tasks that you will *not* want to have decided without your input, such as which of your systems are critical and which are not.

Defining the tasks carefully allows you to control the amount of time and dollars that the consultant may insist are needed to manage the project. While your estimates may not end up being entirely accurate, you will start with an idea of the time and dollars you can afford. This will help in your discussions with the consultant as well as your negotiating position. If, in fact, it winds up being more expensive than you think, it is far better to know that *before* the project starts, rather than 90% of the way through your money and only 50% through the program.

2. Finding candidates

Start the process the same way you might start a search for any other consultant: talk to your business associates, banker, lawyer, and accountant to see if they can recommend anyone or have any contacts.

Your accountant may already offer year 2000 services, and this may be an optimum solution, but be cautious! Some accountants may be very good with financial systems, but may not have the practical experience to deal with upgrading your inventory systems and handle your sales and marketing programs. On the other hand, some large accounting firms may have a number of junior consultants who can work quite well under the supervision of a senior staffer, and this size of firm will also have the depth of other resources should you need them.

Many small businesses will come to the conclusion that they are more interested in hiring a project manager. This might be someone who can come in one day a week or twice a month to make sure that all the pieces of the plan are proceeding on schedule and that specific tasks are getting done, and who can assist other staff on an as-needed basis. Note that there are a number of project management associations that may be able to provide membership lists, or it may be worthwhile to go to some of their meetings and see if you can establish personal contact.

There are many excellent small companies out there that can tackle your project and complete it professionally and at a very competitive price. Just keep in mind that they are often new companies and, despite excellent technical qualifications, they may rarely be able to offer many references of successfully completed projects. But beware of the con artist! (Section c. discusses this issue further.)

3. Setting the criteria

Table #3 shows a list of questions you may want to ask your candidates. Not all may apply; some depend on the size of your problem and the range of choices you may have about who you can hire. You should add your own questions that deal specifically with the challenges faced by your company.

Above all, you must stay involved with the year 2000 project as much as possible: don't hand it off to a third party and assume that you have now solved the issue. It is potentially your business that is at risk; you cannot afford to leave it in the hands of outsiders, no matter what the reputation and skills they bring to addressing this issue.

4. Signing a contract

In almost every case when you deal with an outside firm, you will sign a contract for the goods or services that it will deliver. Typically the contract will include penalties if these goods and services are not delivered according to the contract's terms. However, the year 2000 is a special case. "Close" isn't good enough; if your systems are not working properly by January 1, 2000, your costs will be huge and could potentially mean the end of your business. Many year 2000 consultants will refuse to sign a contract with such absolute requirements. Understand clearly that they already have more work than they can deal with; the risk of walking away from a contract may be no risk at all.

Gregory Cirillo, a lawyer with Williams, Mullen, Christian & Dobbins in the United States, has written a number of articles on year 2000 contracts. A summary of his advice, from his article "Y2K Remediation Contracts: When Your Back is Against the Wall," is given below.

You have to realize that what you want to buy is as much the *process* as the end product. Certainly you want complete and compliant systems working at the end of all your efforts, but if for any reason the process gets halted in midstream,

TABLE #3
QUESTIONS TO ASK PROSPECTIVE CONSULTANTS

1. How long have you been in business?
2. How long have you been in the year 2000 business?
3. How many other offices do you have?
4. Do you have consultants dedicated to this specialty?
5. How big is your consulting staff?
6. Do you have partners or alliances that can also provide specialized personnel if needed?
7. Do you follow a standard methodology? (There are a number on the market that may apply.)
8. Can you provide resources outside of this country (if you run an international operation)?
9. Do you have alliances with any specialized year 2000 solution providers?
10. Do you have access to any special software or tool sets to help you with the problem?
11. How well do you understand the workings of the industry?
12. What business experience can you point to outside of information technology?
13. Can you give me a list of references?
14. Can you give me a list of your technical qualifications and credentials?

you must be able to pick up and carry on from that point. You do not have the time to go back to the start and begin again.

If this is the case, then your contract should be precise about all the parts of the process that you are buying. This should include:

(a) the number of people dedicated exclusively to your contract,

(b) a limit on turnover, subject to your approval (this is to limit the consultant constantly substituting resources), and

(c) the number of days or hours of each person working on the contracts.

You may also wish to talk to the consultant about his or her own staff turnover, and whether he or she provides any control through the use of non-competition clauses. As prices escalate, the temptation for individuals to jump ship will become ever greater, even if your consultant remains committed to you. One option you may want to examine is employing the personnel directly. This means you may have a greater ability to retain personnel even if you have to change consultants. On the other hand, it may be just as hard to hang on to them, and you may not have the time to spend on legal remedies should your new staff defect.

If for any reason the contract does terminate prematurely, there are some key clauses that will help you maintain the maximum amount of control over the ongoing operations of the year 2000 conversion team:

(a) First, the contract should specify that all work in process, including logs and records of your property, will be left with you if and when the contract is terminated.

(b) Second, the consultant should give you the license for any tools or techniques purchased, so that these are not lost to you if the contractor walks away from the project.

(c) Third, the contract should specify a post-termination transition period during which the consultant's personnel remains on site or available for consultation.

You may also want to try and work in a provision that allows you to approach the consulting firm's staff to remain in your employ after termination. This final suggestion may be the most controversial, because it will be contrary to the typical situation where you agree *not* to hire away the vendor's personnel.

All of the above points discuss the remedies you need to control should the contract fail. A better situation is the one where there are no problems in the first place. The best way of obtaining this is through hands-on, full-time contract management by your staff. This is yet another reason why your company's year 2000 coordinator needs to have this project as a first priority. The coordinator cannot manage the process at all if his or her main activity is to read written reports well after consultants have made and acted on decisions. It also makes little sense not to have an individual with a detailed knowledge of the company's operations working hand in hand with the conversion experts on a day-to-day basis.

Finally, you should make sure that any problems are addressed and resolved as fast as possible. These may be about priorities to be set, the way systems work, or what the best form of integration may be. If the issues are specifically related to your contractual obligations or those of the consultants, it is in neither party's best interest to let such problems fester and grow. Ongoing communication, both up and down the chain of command, will help prevent any minor misunderstandings from developing into major problems.

c. CAUTION! CAUTION! CAUTION!

In the discussion above, we have talked about two kinds of consultants: those who offer programming and information technology skills, and those who provide more in the way of project management services. There *may* be enough of the latter. There will certainly NOT be enough of the former.

At the time of writing in August 1997, most of the large IT specialists and systems integrators are already working at near capacity and some are turning away business. This is largely because all of their personnel are working at capacity and firms are unable to find additional human resources.

Nevertheless, most of these professional consulting firms are very concerned about those companies that they are unable to help. In my conversations with senior consulting firm executives, several of them expressed the fear that it was medium-sized companies that were most at risk. Businesses in this category, with several hundred employees and revenues in the tens of millions of dollars, often have large in-house systems running on mini-computers or even mainframes. They frequently do not use off-the-shelf software and so need specialists to repair their operating systems. However, these specialists are now fully occupied fixing someone else's problems.

The choices left to such mid-sized companies will often be to hire individuals or consulting companies with little or no track record. While many of these will genuinely try to do the best possible job, there will also be many charlatans and con artists. They will promise the moon for an exorbitant price and then will instantly disappear once it becomes evident that they are not going to succeed, thus leaving their clients worse off than before.

The only advice I have to offer in this case is extreme caution! While you may not have much choice in the resources you can find, always keep the long-range goals of the company in mind. Working inefficiently and with a lot of manual processes through the first part of the year 2000 or even 2001 will be better than not working at all. You must make absolutely sure that your year 2000 coordinator is sufficiently informed and has sufficient authority to step in whenever he or she feels that the company's operations are at risk. Your coordinator must never leave the potential life of the business in the hands of outside consultants.

12
TAKING STOCK

There are four steps involved in implementing any plan:

(a) Collecting as much information as possible

(b) Evaluating your options

(c) Choosing and establishing your plan

(d) Executing your plan

It is no different with your year 2000 project. However, in this case, you have the added complication at the execution stage of having a number of initiatives moving forward simultaneously on several fronts.

The first step, collecting the information, is the subject of this chapter. You must compile a complete and thorough inventory of your hardware, software, and related machinery and equipment, as well as a complete list of all of your systems. You should also include processes currently carried out on the side, such as reports generated via spreadsheets. You may also want to put together a wish list identifying operations that need automatic processing, reports that need to be made, processes that can be streamlined, or other upgrades that would boost your systems' overall efficiency.

Do not underestimate the time that it will take to establish this baseline inventory. If you have a number of departments and limited resources, the inventory section alone, although it might only take an additional day or two, may have to be fitted in over a two- or three-week period. It would be wise for senior management to emphasize the importance of taking inventory and stress the priority of the year 2000 project.

a. COMPUTER HARDWARE

First, you need to make a comprehensive list of all your hardware. This will take a fair amount of time, because you may have to open up each computer to get some of the names and chip numbers and any add-on cards, such as those with extended memory, specialized graphics display, or direct fax capability. You might be able to avoid this step by using software that can identify this information.

If your computers are networked, you must include in your inventory the hubs, routers, switches, and NIC (network interface connector) cards. You may find you have as many of these items as individual computers.

For computer hardware, you should collect the following information:

- Manufacturer
- Model number
- All appropriate serial numbers
- BIOS (basic input/output system) manufacturer
- BIOS version number
- Processor type (e.g., 486, 586)
- Function served (e.g., server, stand-alone)

Gathering this information will give you what you need for your year 2000 project, which is about 80% of all the information you *could* collect. I suggest that for many organizations, it will be worth spending the extra time to get the other 20% — including information about other assets, e.g., furniture and vehicles — to wind up with a list that is truly accurate and complete.

Make sure that you also collect all available information about all the peripheral devices you have scattered through the office. You will have a number of printers, of course, but you may also have equipment such as scanners, backup tapes, plotters, modems, and other devices for input or output. As I suggested earlier, if you are going to take the necessary time to do this inventory, you may as well do it right.

All of this information should be entered into a spreadsheet. Not only is this an easy way of accumulating the data, but it also allows you to group and analyze the information effectively so you can identify how many computers with a certain processor you have, or how many from a particular manufacturer.

b. SOFTWARE

You also need to collect all the information about software packages. You may want to do this at the same time as gathering the hardware information, or you may want to do it as a separate exercise.

Hopefully, you have all the software packages kept in a single location, preferably under lock and key. Start by listing what's there. (The purpose of this is as much related to year 2000 as it is to establish the software licenses you hold. If you are like most businesses, you will almost certainly find that you are using the software in ways and in numbers beyond what is permitted by the licenses you have purchased.)

Once you have this preliminary list, you need to go through each computer and list what is on each machine. The information required for this part of the inventory is as follows:

- Operating system, with version number
- Application, vendor, version number
- Company-built programs (i.e., your own programming)

Again, this information should be accumulated in a separate spreadsheet to allow for later analysis.

You will probably find a good deal of personal software on some computers, as well as software that no one knows anything about. Few computer users regularly clean up their systems and the data and applications on them. This is particularly the case if they are linked together in a local area network (LAN). Often in this case, central storage will tend to mean that individuals save every scrap of information and never have to worry about clearing it out and minimizing the amount of space they take up.

Finding "other" programs on computers provides you with an opportunity to review your software licenses. It is highly likely that you have no right to run these programs. You can use your inventory to help you decide whether you are going to buy a legitimate copy of a particular application, or whether you are going to erase it from the hard disk.

c. SYSTEMS

Next, you should list the systems you use. Note that this is different from the list of software, which is a list of applications only. For example, the software you own could be FoxPro or dBase. But the *system* you may be running on it could vary from order entry to inventory control and customer information. And you may well have several systems that all use the same software.

One of the fallacies maintained by computer professionals (especially those who deny that the year 2000 problem is such a major event) is that everyone upgrades their software all the time. I have read a number of articles about the year 2000 problem that say that since no one has software that is older than three years, the year 2000 issue will not occur. However, businesspeople who operate in the real world know that this is not the case. Many small companies operate their inventory or customer databases quite happily on dBase II or III. They may still use Lotus 2.01 from the days before GUI (graphical user interfaces). Those who are using Windows 3.1 for Workgroups have had no reason (until year 2000 came along) to trade up. And hundreds of thousands of users still use DOS commands to organize their directories and simple front-end menu systems to move between programs.

For some companies, compiling a list of systems may be very simple; perhaps an accounting system is the only system that a company uses in its business. Other enterprises will have order entry systems, personal information managers (PIMs), sales databases, production control systems, routing and scheduling systems for their vehicles, etc.

When you are making up the list of systems, you should also talk to every computer user. Over the years, many companies have found that the particular accounting or inventory package they have purchased did not do everything they wanted it to. Off-the-shelf software by its nature tends to be generic rather than specifically appropriate for every company. If a program did not provide some particular information or a specific report that someone needed, the usual solution has been to build something to work around this situation. This usually has meant developing something in another package, usually a spreadsheet.

It is important that you identify this information. Not only is this another mini-system that you should document, but it also defines a shortcoming of one of your present systems. First, it may surprise you how much you are still using the old dBase III software, for example, that is sitting on someone's computer in a back office. And if the reports generated by this software are critical to good management decisions, you *must* factor its use into your overall systems evaluation. Second, should you decide to replace some of your systems, you should have a full understanding of all your present system's weaknesses and shortcomings — apart from its lack of year 2000 compatibility.

d. OTHER EQUIPMENT AND MACHINERY

Don't forget all the "non-computer" equipment — the various devices around the office and the shop floor that contain embedded computer chips — in your inventory. We have already discussed the telephone PBX system you may own, but there are many other types of equipment that you need to identify.

Your voice mail system may be separate from your PBX system, and you should also consider alarm systems, postage machines, and photocopiers. If you have any other appliances that keep track of usage through a key-entry system of some kind, these too may be vulnerable. Fax machines, for example, date-stamp all incoming and outgoing faxes.

If you are involved in manufacturing at all, you will have a whole other category of machinery that needs to be documented. Particularly if the machinery is at all linked with computers, you will find that a great many pieces of production equipment have some kind of function that is date sensitive. And even if there is only one machine that is date sensitive, if you do not identify it and deal with it, it might bring the whole production line to a standstill.

e. CUSTOMERS AND SUPPLIERS

Finally, you need to accumulate for your plan a comprehensive listing of all of your customers and suppliers.

In the case of suppliers, you will have to be in contact with them to make sure that they too are aware of the problem and are taking the necessary steps to become year 2000 compliant. After all, you need to understand that your own sources of supply are electronically uncontaminated and will provide reliable and ongoing delivery of their goods or services. In the case of customers, a more subtle approach is to find out whether the year 2000 problem will adversely affect their operations, which could cause problems in their ability to pay you.

Many companies keep a vast amount of information about customers and suppliers, but this information is rarely accumulated in one place. Indeed, it is an axiom among competitive intelligence professionals that 80% of the information you need is probably somewhere already within your company. The accounting system will have some information — company name and address — and sales and marketing some more — contact names and phone and fax numbers. Talk to your shipping department in case goods are actually delivered to a different address than the one on the invoice.

This information can be entered into spreadsheets, but you may prefer to look into whether there is a more efficient application that can be used, such as a database, personal information manager, or groupware. The appropriate program ready depends on who has to use the information and the purpose of using it. You need to consider information maintenance; it may be that each department need only work with what it has on record already. Keeping a centralized registry may involve more work than it's worth. Certainly keeping everything in one spot and then allowing it to become out of date — and less easy to access — is not a useful exercise.

You will, however, have to collect all of the various parts together on at least one occasion for the purposes of your year 2000 communications plan (see chapter 16). Make sure that you list all of a company's contacts, not just one. Just as you are your firm's year 2000 champion, you must find the person in this position for each of your suppliers and customers. And that person may not be the accounting manager or the executive in charge of sales, so you should not restrict your list from the outset until you have established who your primary Y2K contact will be.

When you list all of your contacts, be sure to include their titles or positions. It may well be that as your year 2000 plan progresses, there may be some specialized communication between your production manager and your supplier, or your marketing people may want to discuss a combined campaign. If you have built the information in the first place, it will be easy to make these matches as required. If you can, as you accumulate the information, try and look a little farther down the road so that the effort you spend can deliver other benefits beyond those related to year 2000.

f. INVENTORY ALERT! CONSIDERATIONS FOR SPECIALIZED PRODUCTS

During your inventory, you may run into some "non-standard" systems and applications that need to be addressed. In this case, you may wish to call in a specialist.

1. Specialized software issues

(a) No source code

If you have had any specialized programs built for your company, both the internal person who planned the program as well as the external programmer who wrote it may be long gone. In many cases, if the program is an old one, you may be running on compiled code, i.e., a program that the computer generated from the original programs. If you are using these kinds of systems, your best option is probably to start from scratch. One source estimates that in the United States, there is over $50 billion worth of software operating for which no source code exists.

(b) Outdated programming languages

You may find that you have programs and/or data that are in a programming language that either you do not use any more or are not supported by the manufacturer in any way. You may be able to just discard this information, but you should make sure this is the case before you dump it. Unfortunately, older programming languages rarely considered the need to share information, so they may not have even the simplest methods built in to export the data.

Remember too that even if you don't keep the old program, the fact that it exists may help define some of the criteria you must establish for any new systems, whether it defines data collection, processes, or reports.

(c) Application upgrades

Perhaps you find that some of the software you use is out of date, which probably means that you have stopped paying for any form of ongoing support. You will have to decide whether you wish to upgrade these packages, if indeed that is even possible. Some software manufacturers may not be interested in making old programs year 2000 compliant. They may not be able to afford to supply costly upgrades and the potential liabilities they hold; it's just a losing proposition in terms of revenue.

At the same time, make sure that the upgrade will solve your year 2000 problems. If you are using dBase III with a lot of custom code, it may not run on dBase V, so paying for the upgrade may not be the solution.

(d) "Black box" syndrome

You may discover that you have systems about which no one knows anything! These may be stand-alone programs or they may act as bridges between two or more separate systems. You may be able to discard them, but *triple* check before you do. After all, if no one knows what it does, there is probably no one who knows exactly what it will affect when you close it down. And if it crosses departmental boundaries, analyzing this process will be difficult.

2. Specialized systems issues

(a) Archived and tape data

If your company has had computers for a long time, your backup and off-site storage procedures should be well established. It is quite possible, however, that for a variety of reasons, you may access this information on a regular basis, perhaps for looking for information about historical transactions or for analyzing sales trends.

If you use data from the last two years only, you may not have to worry about it being year 2000 compliant if you convert your systems immediately. By the time the new century arrives, the two years of history you need will be held in the new program, not the old ones. But if you use data that is older than this, you will need to look at your options. These may range from converting data, rekeying it, or changing your procedures so you do not look as far back as you do at present.

Another issue that a large company may need to consider is the cost of storage. With your year 2000 conversions, you may be making many more copies of backups than you do at present, and for a large enterprise, storage of these backups may be a significant cost.

(b) Testing difficulties

Whether you continue to use old programs, change some of them, or change all of them, testing the new configuration will be a challenge. For the year 2000 problem, whole books have been written on this subject alone. Some of the issues with which you will have to deal are as follows:

- *The setup of test data.* Should it be old data rekeyed so you can compare it with historical results, or should it be new data because old information won't work?
- *Integration of systems.* If something crashes, what system is not working properly?
- *Timing.* Do you have time to test all systems separately and then retest them when they are all linked together?
- *Volume.* How much do you need to test to be sure that everything is perfect?

The larger the company, the more time testing will take. Testing is a specialized area, so if you don't have the resources within your organization, call in the experts! You cannot afford to spend all of your time and effort upgrading your systems, fudging the testing, and then finding out that all of the new processes don't work.

g. SUMMARY

Some companies will have all of this information readily available in their present systems and the inventory will be done in a few minutes — it will just be a matter of pulling the information. If you are in this position, you are to be congratulated.

In reality, few companies keep truly comprehensive records. This may be because personnel and procedures have changed over the years and something that was inventoried one year may not have been counted the next. It may also be because of accounting procedures that write off everything under a certain dollar amount. For example, your $150 modem may have been expensed in the year it was bought, and so it was not tracked under your list of assets. But you need to identify it in a year 2000 database because if it is date sensitive, your systems may not work until it is fixed.

A comprehensive listing of *all* of your assets is something your bank and insurance company would welcome. In fact, it can probably help you in your day-to-day operations. So go ahead and complete the list. You may be surprised to find what you own!

13
THE THREE Rs: REPAIR, REPLACE, RETIRE

You may be thinking that your analysis will show what is problematic in your operations, but it may show just the opposite. In other words, a system that is critical, but which can easily be replaced, may be less of an overall problem than one that is only slightly less important but will take an enormous amount of work to repair.

This chapter addresses the three options available to solve your problems, to repair, replace, or retire old systems and equipment. In order to establish priorities for implementing your plan, you must weigh the advantages and disadvantages of each choice. Retiring an operation can include outsourcing it entirely to a third party that can provide year 2000 certified services. If an outsider can run it more efficiently and at a better price than you can in-house, that may be the way to go. For example, you might find you can contract out your warehousing or marketing functions.

a. HOW TO MAKE THE CHOICE

1. Hardware

These choices will apply to all the items in your inventory but some are easier to make than others. Hardware decisions should be the easiest of all. For example, you may be able to *repair* your 486 computer by inserting a new BIOS (basic input/output system) chip. If you cannot fix it, you may have to *replace* the function that it performs in that particular location with a new computer. And if you cannot do that in such a way that there is no risk to any other system, you will have to *retire* it.

In this case, you can decide by looking at the facts. A replacement chip is either available or not available. But the choice becomes more complicated when you start looking at software, and will involve even more judgment in your systems analysis.

2. Software

For small enterprises, you may not consider that the repair option will be used a great deal. Repair, after all, is a more appropriate solution when you have invested in thousands or millions of lines of code, and smaller companies are much more likely to rely on off-the-shelf programs. But if you extend the definition of repair to include upgrades, then certainly you may pursue this route.

Unfortunately, it is medium-sized companies that may have the most problems with their software systems. Many of these enterprises often have sophisticated systems developed over years of operation and rarely rely on off-the-shelf solutions. I say "unfortunately" because they may need professional programming help to adjust their systems, and unless they have started already, they may find that they are unable to locate any information technology professionals who can help them within the time frame required.

Both small- and medium-sized companies should not ignore the repair option, however. You may have a number of smaller systems that have been built for internal purposes over the years, and they might include the use of spreadsheets, databases, or even word processing programs to generate information and reports not available through other traditional application packages. If you do decide to continue the practice of generating information through this method, repair could be as easy as upgrading your Excel spreadsheets to the latest version from Microsoft.

3. Systems

Upgrading your operating system is one of the more obvious steps you can take to help avoid the year 2000 problem. Particularly if you are DOS-based (perhaps with a menu between you and the operating system), but even if you are operating Windows for Workgroups 3.x, you should definitely consider moving all of your operating systems up to Windows 95. This is because Windows 95, and applications that operate through this front end, rely on the operating clock of the software rather than the internal hardware clock to establish the date. Within Windows 95, the system can handle the year date "00." Within Windows for Workgroups and other operating systems, you are dependent on computer chips that may not be able to interpret "00" correctly. Better still, wait for Windows 98 or Memphis, which Microsoft says will be completely Y2K compliant.

b. REPAIR

1. **Advantages**
- Repair will usually involve a shorter time frame and carry fewer risks than replacement.
- Repair takes advantage of your existing programs, essentially keeping in place a tried-and-true system.

2. **Disadvantages**
- Repair may still be an expensive route to follow. The analysis of your existing code and its correction can probably be done only by experts, and this will cost a lot of money.
- You remain committed to following existing policy and procedures. In other words, you are taking your existing methodology and continuing to work with it into the 21st century.
- Repairs may be harder to test. In most cases, you will be testing your existing systems. With some added patches, it may be possible that a correction won't be made in a certain field and yet the whole system will appear to work well.

Upgrades may also solve the problems, if any, of many of your standard application packages, e.g., accounting programs. One of the leading accounting packages, Great Plains, has already released its year 2000 compliant version. If you are already using Great Plains, or its Windows version called Dynamics, the repair solution may be a "no-brainer" for your accounting department. Should you decide to follow this route, you may be accepting a solution that allows you to keep doing the same processes, and may produce the same set of reports that you were getting before (this may be good or bad, depending on your present satisfaction level). This will vary from package to package, as upgrades typically offer more than a fix of previous bugs.

3. Alternative repair

There are a number of specialized techniques for making repairs to custom-written code. These range from expanding the standard six-digit field to eight digits, converting the six digits to a number so that 1 represents January 1, 1900, 2 represents January 2, 1900, and so on, or even treating the dates as negative or positive to determine which century it belongs to!

The two most popular alternative repair methods are *date windowing*, also know as *mirroring*, and *program encapsulation*, also called the *28-year adjustment*.

Windowing is a process whereby a window of a hundred years is installed in between the data entry point and the program. A small sub-routine then takes all year fields, for instance from 00 to 49, and assumes that they are in the 21st century, while all dates from 50 to 99 are assumed to be in the 20th century. The window then interprets all the dates input and outputs according to this logic, and then adjusts the transactions accordingly.

This method can work quite well providing that you have no data that falls outside of the window. However, if you have data going back to 1901, then you really can't use such an adjustment technique. The other problem is that essentially, it's only a temporary fix. Though some might argue that "temporary" can mean 20 or 30 years, this is the kind of logic that got us into the year 2000 mess in the first place! Also, it won't solve the problem posed by birth dates.

The 28-year adjustment offers an interesting twist on the repair option, although it's one that can be applied only to large systems. The days of the week, corrected for the variations caused by leap years, repeat themselves every 28 years (a seven-day schedule times a four-year leap year schedule). There is a company in the United States that has developed a fix for large programs. Instead of making sure that every possible date field is expanded to include the century, it makes sure that all date calculations are intercepted before they can cause any problems.

Under this scenario, a computer program is adjusted so that the year 2000, for example, is altered before it goes into the program to read 1972. The computer then performs its processes as it would have 28 years ago, and then produces the answer. Any calculations that are done if the year has been input as greater than 2000 then have 28 years added to the result when it exits from the computer in order to adjust them back again.

It is an interesting solution that may help buy time if traditional repair processes take too long. The fact that we all become 28 years younger may also help sell this particular year 2000 solution!

The bottom-line is that there are a number of techniques you can use to adjust dates, so don't accept advice that there is only one possible way to repair your system. All of the choices, however, will require expert help, and this is an issue with which medium-sized companies will have to wrestle more than small enterprises.

c. REPLACE

Replacement may appear to be an easier solution, and perhaps it is in the long run. However, do not underestimate the amount of time and effort that a brand new system will take, especially if you are trying to reorganize processes and change job descriptions at the same time that you maintain your current system.

If your systems are not adequate at present and you have decided to follow the replacement route, be aware that the investigation and research of your systems will take a considerable amount of time and effort. Regardless of the internal resources you can apply, you will depend on the timely response of outside vendors before you can start developing your option short lists.

If, however, you are not satisfied with your current systems and procedures, it is almost certain that replacement will be your best solution if you choose the right package. On the other hand, replacement almost invariably will take more time than repair. This is particularly true if you are trying to integrate the systems of two related but totally separate departments, such as accounting and sales. Here you are dealing not only with two different sets of priorities but two different cultures, and the learning curve for both to understand the other's needs may be too much to absorb and solve in the time available.

As January 1, 2000, draws near, this option may become less attractive if you cannot guarantee that you will meet all of your deadlines. On the other hand, it could be that repair of a critical system is impossible, while replacement may still offer the faint chance of success.

1. **Advantages**

- Replacement optimizes all of your systems by introducing the latest technologies. You'll be able to bridge existing gaps, produce the information presently missing, as well as improve interfaces while making your entire system more reliable and cohesive.

- Replacement may be cheaper in terms of absolute financial outlay, though the time put in by your existing staff may be considerable.

- Replacement may be an easier sell to senior management, if for no other reason than the business benefits are more obvious and tangible. Repair tends to offer expenditures with no substantial improvements.

2. **Disadvantages**
- Given your limited time frame, replacement may carry higher risks than repair or retirement. Do not underestimate the time it will take to do the research, let alone the implementation.
- Replacement may be unnecessary. Or are you imposing a huge burden on your staff merely to get one or two reports that are currently missing?

If you do decide to replace your system, double and triple check that the new package is, indeed, year 2000 compliant.

d. RETIRE

In their systems analysis, large enterprises often deal with hundreds of programs that have been developed over the decades. They often find that some of these programs have no discernible value and can be abandoned. For example, the U.S. Department of Defense is reportedly going to let over 600 systems die on January 1, 2000.

It is far less likely for small- and medium-sized enterprises to have a large number of programs whose purpose is so unclear that they can be just dropped. On the other hand, particularly if the "replace" option is adopted for a number of systems, it may well be that the new systems will replace functions of others to the point where these other existing systems can indeed be retired.

1. **Advantages**
- It's the cheapest solution, effectively zero cost.

2. **Disadvantages**
- There is the possibility of significant risk. Are you absolutely sure that this system has no value?

e. OUTSOURCING

Outsourcing may be an attractive solution if you're considering retiring systems, particularly as time grows shorter. Even without the year 2000 problem, companies have been looking at all of their processes to see whether they are being conducted at peak efficiency, particularly those that include recording and reporting functions. Many companies have found that some of these functions can be better done by a third party that specializes in that function.

Other companies in your industry may also be considering outsourcing certain operations if a suitable supplier can be found. If such a service does not exist today, it may be an opportunity for a new company to offer a consistent and comprehensive service to several companies in the same industry.

1. **Advantages**
- Outsourcing may be safer because the risk is transferred along with the operation.

2. **Disadvantages**
- You may be transferring skill sets from your own employees to workers outside the company.

- You must be positive about the other party's reliability, or have contingency plans in place to lessen the risk. If you have to do this, you lose much of your advantage.

14
GETTING YOUR INVENTORY IN SHAPE

Now it is time to identify your risk, chip by chip, so to speak. Using the inventory databases you have established, you need to discover which equipment is compliant and which is not. Some of the work will be done through more fact gathering, some will require subjective judgment.

Remember to take advantage of the sorting capabilities of the spreadsheets you have used to collect all of the information. Sort the computers by manufacturer to help you systematically go through each checking procedure. Then re-sort them according to their network cards and again check their possible faults. In this way, one phone call may get the answers to the technical problems of a number of units.

Remember, too, as you sort through your information, your choices of either repairing, replacing, or retiring any piece of equipment. Certainly it may be possible to find a year 2000 compliant chip that will fit in that older 386 computer you are still using. But is it really worth the time and effort to do so? Right now, the 386 is already old technology and there are still two years to go before January 1, 2000. Is it realistic to think you will still be using it at that time?

a. HARDWARE

You have your list of all the equipment you own that may be affected by the millennium bug. Now you have to check it out, piece by piece.

There are three time-keeping "players" in a PC:

(a) The BIOS (basic input output system), which controls the interface between the operating system and the PC hardware

(b) The RTC (real time clock), which functions as a running clock and a keeper of two-digit year values

(c) The CMOS (complementary metal oxide semiconductor), a memory chip that stores the RTC data

If any of these three parts malfunctions, or if the interface between the parts does not work properly, the computer will not be able to process year 2000 dates. And remember that almost half of the computers being sold *today* are not going to work without problems in the year 2000. Don't assume that you can skip over your Pentium or other 586 technology.

1. Computer chips

Once you have the manufacturer name and number of each of the three chips listed above, you must contact them to find out whether each is year 2000 compliant. A number of the larger chip manufacturers have Web sites where you can get the information you need. In other cases you may have to talk to someone on the phone. Any information given to ~~you over the~~ phone is less reliable, because it can be denied later. Ask for the information to be put in writing in all cases (see section e. below).

Another way of checking year 2000 compatibility is to use some of the software available. There are an increasing number of testing programs available on the Internet. Although some programs will do initial tests as shareware, at no charge, many of them charge a fee for the full version. Prices are often reasonable (under $100), and may include some software fixes for that price as well. HighSpin tries to maintain a current list of such programs on its Web site (www.highspin.com), as do some of the other year 2000 Web pages.

Investing in this kind of software may well be worthwhile. The biggest cost to a company for this part of its evaluation will be time, so if $100 can save you two or three hours, it is probably worth it. For companies that have more than three to five computers, you may save far more time than that.

2. Fixing the chips

Having found out which of your chips needs to be fixed, you must now find out how and whether you can fix it. You may find there are *software fixes* that will allow you to go in and correct the chip without having to replace it. This is ideal, and if these fixes come from the manufacturer, you can be reasonably sure of their effectiveness. There are also some excellent third-party fixes available.

In any attempted conversion of this type, *back up everything first!* Even if you are dealing with a brand-name supplier and a brand-name fix, don't assume that it will work perfectly. One element that will work perfectly on both sides of the millennium is Murphy's Law.

If you cannot fix your chip by reprogramming, your only solution may be to buy a replacement chip. Again, the best place to obtain such a replacement will be from the original manufacturer, but in many cases you may find that the manufacturer is impossible to locate. This may be because it has gone out of business, but it may also be that it has changed its name, merged with another firm, or been bought out by a competitor that no longer supports that chip.

If you have to use third-party suppliers, a good place to find them listed is in the classified sections of computer magazines. The publication with the largest lists of such suppliers is probably *Computer Shopper*, an inch-thick magazine available at most good book and magazine stores. "Buyer Beware!" is still the order of the day in such circumstances, but it may be the only solution left to you, short of junking the computer entirely.

b. SOFTWARE

In exactly the same way that you deal with your hardware inventory, you can now proceed with your software list. For many companies using standard software, this may be a much more straightforward process and easier to evaluate. Remember though that even if an application can be made year 2000 compliant, this compliancy does not necessarily fix the actual system you are running on top of that application, particularly if you have developed custom code over the years.

For example, dBase V is year 2000 compliant, and the older dBase III software application can be upgraded to the more modern version. However, this does not mean that the order entry system that you had written four years ago will necessarily move along that upgrade path without some reprogramming. This is a question for systems analysis, which is covered in chapter 15.

Incidentally, now may be a good time to organize the company's overall software programs. While this is not strictly a year 2000 issue, you may as well take advantage of the opportunity. This certainly means updating all appropriate licenses so that you meet your legal responsibilities. It may also mean just making sure that everyone is using the same version of the software. You may be surprised to find out how much time you have been wasting converting files forwards and backwards to match the software versions on different computers. Now too may be the time to unify your software into a single suite, whether WordPerfect, Lotus, or Microsoft.

Finally, you should take a look at all of the other programs that you didn't know were even on your computers. There may be utilities or other helpers you can use and you should consider buying the latest version. On the other hand, if you decide to stop their use, be sure to delete them from all the hard drives.

You may have read that Macintoshes and other Apple computers are not affected by the year 2000 bug. In general, this is true for Apple hardware. It is not necessarily true for Apple-based software. Many of these programs come from third-party suppliers, and have often been "ported" from PC versions. While many of them may be year 2000 compliant, probably a higher percentage than PCs, you cannot assume there is no risk, and you should check them out.

---

c. OTHER HARDWARE COMPONENTS

There is an equal amount of effort required to check all of the other hardware components you have identified in your inventory. You may be able to cut down the amount of work involved by considering the use to which the computer is put and whether it is part of a network.

For example, a 386 computer that you use for word processing may operate perfectly well in the new millennium provided it does no date sensitive calculations *and* is not in contact with any other computers whose operations it may affect. In the long run you will definitely have to fix it or replace it, but it makes sense to focus on the critical elements of your hardware. Spend time on the less important components of your business operation *after* January 1, 2000. It makes sense in terms of the best use of your limited staff and time resources to double check that you constantly remain focused on the critical components.

Checking other hardware components may be more difficult because most of us are less familiar with network cards, routers, and modems than we are with the actual PC. Many smaller companies use a third-party supplier to set up their network, their connection to the Internet, and any interoffice communication systems. If you can, use that third party to check out the year 2000 compatibility of the components it installed. If you cannot, you will have to follow up by phone.

d. NON-COMPUTER EQUIPMENT

Just as for computer equipment, you will need to check the year 2000 compliancy of the items on your non-computer equipment list. This list will likely be shorter, but the problem you may face is that some manufacturers will not have developed standard procedures for answering enquiries about whether their equipment will work in the new millennium.

Remember, for example, that the card reader that is attached to your photocopier to track who uses what copies for what project may not come from the photocopier manufacturer. It may have been installed by a third party, and it is this company with whom you will have to confirm year 2000 compatibility.

The biggest cost you may incur in this category of equipment is with your phone system. Many of the PBX systems come from the larger telecommunications firms, and of all industries, this may be one of the most year 2000 aware. However, in many cases you may not be able to just buy a replacement chip, but instead will have to upgrade the phone system. These manufacturers often offer a fairly large percentage discount to existing customers, but the overall investment required may still be in the range of several thousand dollars.

e. GET IT IN WRITING — EVERY TIME!

When you have to rely on the information provided over the phone from the program manufacturer concerning year 2000 compliance, you often encounter flip reassurances that naturally their equipment will work perfectly well into the next millennium. If you receive this kind of response, the absolute rule that you must follow every time is GET IT IN WRITING!

> In an interesting evaluation, a U.K.-based company, Greenwich Mean Time, tested more than 4,000 software packages. Of these, only 2,000 claimed to be year 2000 compliant. But more alarming was the discovery that of those 2,000 applications that claimed to have no problems with the millennium bug, more than 700, or over 35%, were in fact *not* year 2000 compliant.

Obtaining confirmation in writing will immediately accomplish two things. First, it will make the person at the other end of the telephone pause. It will also likely result in your request being kicked upstairs to someone with more authority, and hopefully more knowledge. This means that the brusque confirmation to your question will be examined more seriously and an answer provided by someone who understands what you are asking.

Second, it will provide you with documentation that will be very important should you have to go back to the manufacturer in 2000 with any kind of legal claims. A company can always deny what its representative may have said; it cannot do the same with something in writing on company letterhead. Conversely, if the supplier has any business sense, it too will recognize that a written statement constitutes a legal representation. A manufacturer will be much more careful, and likely more accurate, in any written information it gives you.

15
TRIAGE: ESTABLISHING PRIORITIES FOR YOUR SYSTEMS

Triage: The sorting of and allocation of treatment to patients and especially battle and disaster victims according to a system of priorities designed to maximize the number of survivors.

That's how *Webster's* dictionary defines it, but anyone who was a fan of the television program *M*A*S*H** saw it put into action as the doctors and nurses on the show did a quick assessment and moved on the priorities.

It's a pretty good analogy for what's going to have to happen in a lot of businesses over the next couple of years. In this context, triage means the sorting and selection of treatment approaches for date-impacted programs and systems to maximize the number of survivors.

Some possible year 2000 treatments include in-house code repair, outsourced code repair, replacement with a commercial off-the-shelf software package or outsourced solution, and retirement. But to decide which is most applicable, you need to take an overall look at all of the systems you have operating and rate them according to various criteria. Once you have completed the analysis of your systems and applied some priorities, you are in a position to start fixing some of the problems. However, any analysis depends on where you are as a company.

a. WHAT WILL IT MEAN FOR MY BUSINESS?

Your systems analysis may be the one area where everything grinds to a halt. While much of the rest of the process is a matter of establishing facts, any appraisal of which systems and processes are most critical to a business enterprise involves questions of judgment. Your senior managers are bound to differ, if for no other reason than their natural belief in the importance of their own particular department over all the others.

If some of those ideas point in different directions and to different system needs, you will not be able to move forward until you sort out those differences and decide on a unified course. Alternatively, the president or owner will have to make a decision which will allow the company to continue its analysis of its systems, even if it doesn't allow time to achieve complete consensus.

It really helps if you have a formal strategic plan for the company. In fact, this is one of the benefits that the year 2000 challenge can bring. Having such a plan means that the company has already determined the environment in which it operates, as well as decided on particular business directions in which to grow. (A more complete discussion of this opportunity is covered in chapter 17.)

For example, one company may have decided recently that, for a variety of reasons, it no longer wishes to be in the distribution business. This probably means that it will take this formerly in-house function and contract it out to an outside supplier. In the context of the year 2000 problem, this means that it will not waste time discussing whether a software program concerned with managing the company's distribution system should be repaired, replaced, or retired. The decision has already been made within the context of the strategic plan.

Naturally in this example, if the plan doesn't exist yet, the firm will have to spend time analyzing its distribution software system. It may be that it will conclude that this function should be outsourced, and plan accordingly. However, it may decide that it does not have sufficient lead time to consider this option, which may force it to spend time and resources fixing a program that in three years it may not need.

So if you have enough time, the first step in analyzing your systems may be to step back and decide as a company where you are at present and where you are going. In everything involved with year 2000, time is a crucial factor. Your ability to do this planning — which could be the key to a more successful future — may depend on when you are reading this. If it is sometime in 1998 and you operate a small company with few customized systems, taking the time to do some long-range planning for your firm could be tremendously important. This is not only because it is something you should be doing anyway, even if the year 2000 problem hadn't forced the issue. It is also because your decisions about which of your systems are the most important may change if you consider new ways of operating or new markets you might develop.

But if you're reading this late in 1998 or in 1999, don't spend the time on your long-term future without ensuring your more immediate survival. In other words, make the priority decisions *now*, in the present environment, even if they are being made in a partial vacuum. Better to have a company that you can change in the future than to spend too much time deciding how to improve it. On January 1, 2000, you may no longer have a functioning enterprise to make changes in at all.

b. SYSTEMS: SUBJECTIVE ANALYSIS

When it comes to systems, much of the analysis will be subjective, and so the time involved may be spent less in gathering facts than in gathering opinions. These judgments should be applied not only to the systems as they exist at present but also to how you would like them to best operate into the future.

You also need to look at all the initiatives that you have under way to see whether there may be a potential conflict with year 2000 measures. For medium-sized companies which may have a number of improvements or upgrades underway, make sure these initiatives are compatible with your year 2000 plans. For example, don't start coding a new order entry system until you know for certain that the base you are using will remain in place. You may have to modify some projects or even delay or cancel them until your year 2000 issues have been resolved.

In many cases, the future direction of a particular system, department, or even the company as a whole will be subject to change. If you can at least decide whether your present systems can adapt to that change, whether you need to replace them, or whether outsourcing is an option, this will help a great deal in your analysis of each part of the process.

c. CHOOSING THE CRITERIA

Drawing up your inventory provided you with a complete list of all your systems. Hopefully you also have an additional wish list identifying how they could be improved. Now you have to decide which are the most important and which need to be worked on first.

Imagine a company that has only three systems: one for accounting, one for order entry, and a third for production. These systems could be prioritized in three different ways depending on the criteria used.

Which systems are more critical? A failure of the accounting system will eventually mean that the company will go bankrupt due to an inability to manage its cash flows, or so the accounting department will argue. Similarly, the production manager will insist that accounting will be irrelevant if the company cannot produce any goods. Finally, the sales and marketing executive will point out that if he cannot make and record his sales, then both the other systems are redundant. Who's right?

If you look at the systems from the point of view of establishing alternative manual processes, it may be very easy to replace the order entry system with appropriate paper-based systems and the addition of one person working part time. To do the same for the accounting system would be more difficult and would require two additional two staff members. But the production system ties in directly with a number of pieces of equipment on the shop floor that use computer designs to produce the various parts required. It is impossible to reproduce this system manually.

On another level, you may want to evaluate the systems on the basis of improvements that you would like to install. Here, the production system is working perfectly and nothing needs changing. The accounting system is working well, although some of its reporting abilities could be improved, and it would benefit from a direct interface with the order entry system. On the other hand, the order entry system, which is run by the sales department, needs a major overhaul. It is cumbersome, fails to generate the reports needed, takes a long time for training, and the sales people are unable to use it from their homes or regional offices.

As outlined previously, your choices with these three systems are to repair, replace, or retire them. The choice *could* be a simple one. If you have an old system that was custom-built five years ago and the programmer is long gone, the repair option may not exist, and if it is vital to the company, retiring it is not an alternative you can consider.

The point is that there may be a number of criteria that you want to examine, and the importance of each will be weighed differently by different companies. But there are a few key questions:

(a) Is it critical? Could your company operate its business if this system disappeared for a week or a month?

(b) Do I have the manpower, in-house or outside, to do the job in the time available? Do I have the manpower, in-house or outside, to do a manual process for a time after January 1, 2000?

(c) What is my best choice between repairing, replacing, and retiring this process? Does the time available mean that one or more of these choices is probably unworkable?

If you put all of these elements together and apply them to the example given, the results are fairly clear. The production system *must* be repaired, the order entry system can be either retired or replaced, while the accounting system can be replaced or repaired. For the last two systems, there is a large organizational advantage if they work together. Since one of the best options in both cases is replacement, the company should probably research the possibility of finding a brand new system that can offer the best of both worlds to both departments.

This is an easy example; in the real world it may be much more difficult to make such a clear choice. One overwhelming factor may be the amount of time with which you have to work, because there may be a far shorter time line involved with one of the choices than with another. However, this should give you a good idea as to how you should approach the problem, the factors you may have to consider in determining each case, and the fact that you should keep an open mind about your options rather than believing that one approach will serve all systems best.

16
YOUR COMMUNICATIONS PLAN

Like anything else in business, you can't carry out your year 2000 plan in a vacuum. You must communicate that plan to anyone affected by your actions.

There will be two parts to your communication plan: internal and external. The internal plan will inform your staff about the problem and communicate to them what you are planning to do about it. It should be designed to solicit their feedback as well as their active involvement. It also needs to win their *immediate* understanding and support.

The second part of the plan, directed to your customers and your suppliers, is just as important. Early on you may be able to combine messages to these two groups, although at a later date you may wish to treat them somewhat differently.

Your communications campaign will take time and require effort, but if done right — and done early — the benefits you will receive could far outweigh the costs involved.

a. THE INSIDE JOB — COMMUNICATING THE PLAN TO STAFF

Earlier in this book, I devoted considerable space to discussing how the year 2000 problem would affect all aspects of all the operations of your company. You now must use the same set of arguments to convince everyone else in the company that year 2000 is a serious issue and that, yes, it affects each of them and each department.

Expect some resistance to this message. First, you're likely to face the same arguments outlined in chapter 3, so you know how to respond. Since part of the message will be that many employees may have more work thrust upon them because of the crisis, it's natural for them not to embrace the plan immediately.

In other words, it won't an easy sell, which is another reason why strong support from top management, as well as a unified front from all senior executives, is very important in terms of the impression you want to give the rest of the staff. Senior management must all support the year 2000 plan and believe that it is a major business concern for the company.

It is important that you provide enough time for a full discussion of the problem, its implications for everyone attending the meeting, and an outline of the preliminary plan. In my presentations on this subject, in both public forums and private offices, I find that there is at least three hours of material to discuss. Given that your focus will be more specific, it may be possible to cut this time in half, but you should still anticipate another 30 to 60 minutes of questions and discussion.

In this initial meeting, you have a choice between inviting almost all of the company to attend, and inviting just the key people in each department. The disadvantage of the first approach is that you will lose a half-day of work for everyone who attends. If you hold it in the evening or on a weekend, you will cut into their leisure time; this is sure to add to people's resistance to your message.

On the other hand, the disadvantage of the second method is that those employees not "chosen" to attend may resent the exclusive invitation to the meeting. Further, a smaller meeting means you have to rely on those individuals to accurately relay your message to their coworkers. Are you sure they will do that?

There is no correct approach to conveying this communication; it depends very much on the character of the company and the nature of its operations. However, you need to hold this meeting as soon as possible.

You may want to involve an outsider to lead part or all of this discussion. Sometimes an outsider can bring a more objective approach to the topic than an insider, who may be seen as having a "hidden agenda." Your auditor or systems professional may be able to explain the issues in a neutral way that will be more acceptable than if it came from a senior executive.

A disadvantage to using an outsider, though, is that he or she may be seen as carrying an unwelcome message from senior management. As well, if the person doesn't understand the company thoroughly, he or she may not speak in terms that every employee will understand.

I can't emphasize enough how important it is for this meeting to take place, and that it go well. The year 2000 issue is something with which the whole company must be concerned and involved. If one segment of the business does not buy into this message, then at best your overall efforts will be weakened and people will doubt that everyone is putting in maximum effort. At worst, it will mean that your initiatives and action plans will have holes in them, and these could seriously threaten the system changes you need to carry out.

b. GO TELL THE WORLD: COMMUNICATING THE PLAN TO YOUR SUPPLIERS AND CUSTOMERS

A recurring message in this book has been that you cannot solve your year 2000 problem alone. Your suppliers and customers who depend on you, and on whom you depend, are crucial players.

Your existing customers may be unaware of the issue, so your communications to them present an opportunity to show them you are on top of the issue and their business shouldn't be affected. It's a good chance to cement your current relationship.

If your suppliers aren't aware of the problem, you run the risk of not being able to maintain an adequate supply of raw materials, components, or services — a threat to your own business operations.

The balance between suppliers and customers varies by company. A business that sells goods to the public that come from a hundred different overseas suppliers has a different challenge than one that sells services to half a dozen large manufacturers and whose own suppliers are all local.

One factor that may be common to both suppliers and customers is an increased risk to your enterprise if you are dealing with foreign companies. Their awareness of the year 2000 problem is generally far less than in North America, so it will be more difficult to get them involved in the process. Second, communication will be more difficult, hindered by language and time zone differences. Finally, they may be most affected by crashes in their country's systems — government, banks, transportation, and telecommunications. Transportation and telecommunication systems may be operating well in the United States, for example, but I believe there are large risks related to federal government operations, and particularly banks in that country.

1. Plan carefully

There are several good reasons why you should plan your overall communications strategy carefully. The first and most obvious reason is that if your suppliers are not on side, it will be very difficult for you to achieve year 2000 compliance. There are also a number of other reasons, including:

(a) A good communications campaign should have some very strong public relations benefits. If you start it soon, you may be the first company to contact a large number of your customers and suppliers. If you can get the message across well, you may also be able to get coverage from the local media, particularly press and radio. Although the focus of this coverage will naturally be your concern about year 2000, any publicity about your enterprise is bound to boost the overall public awareness of your firm. Besides increasing your community profile, it may well raise your stature in your industry as well.

(b) Consider how you can integrate this initiative with some or all aspects of your overall marketing campaign. For example, one part of your plan might be to host one or more seminars to explain the problem to present and potential customers and suppliers. Whether you give the seminar yourself or whether you hire an outside consultant, this sort of event would give you an excellent reason to invite a number of businesses that might not otherwise come to visit you. Providing year 2000 information in an open forum is a very non-threatening way in which you can provide your potential customers with a valuable service, and at the same time allow you to get to know them a little better.

(c) Developing a successful communications plan may decrease the amount of work you have to do. Particularly in a small community or in a tight industry, you may find that many of the suppliers that you wish to question about year 2000 preparedness will be common to a number of different companies. If you can establish a group committee, you will be able to split the list and the work involved between a number of participants. There may be some extra coordination required, but you will find that communicating about year 2000 is a lengthy and repetitive task, and you should take every opportunity to divide the workload.

The size of your communications campaign, its intensity, the number of people you will have to talk to, and the number of times you will have to repeat your message will vary significantly from business to business. It will depend very much on your company's size and the number of suppliers and customers you have. This may be unrelated to the size; a small company may have many contacts, while some large ones only a few. Whether people accept your message will also have an effect on what you plan to do.

It is impossible to determine how long you will have to conduct this campaign. You may be lucky and find that your approach is not only appreciated, but that a large number of your suppliers are aware of the situation and have already started their own action plans to deal with the problem.

I hope you will be that fortunate. At the other end of the spectrum, you may find many suppliers that refuse to listen to you, that do not believe there is a problem. The problem you will face with this group is deciding how long you are prepared to spend to try and convince them. At some stage, you may have to start searching for new suppliers that can provide you with goods and services that are year 2000 compliant.

2. Suppliers

Depending on your industry, your suppliers may be key partners in your overall business enterprise, and they need to be brought under the umbrella of your year 2000 plan. So, just like your message to your employees, you must spend the time to make sure that they understand the problem and are able to do everything necessary to make the entire process work. It can be a strong win-win situation — you need their year 2000 ready goods and they want your business.

After you've convinced them that *you* are ready, you need to be sure they are, too. You may wish to ask for an outline of their overall plan, ostensibly to help you with your own planning. This will certainly allow you to judge the depth of their preparations. And given the overall uncertainties about the year 2000, I expect that many businesses will be very ready to cooperate and share information for the good of all. That being the case, sharing of plans and commenting on particular problems or solutions may well be the best way of proving that a company is taking the issue seriously.

If your suppliers are not moving ahead with their year 2000 preparations, you may have to get out a stick and start prodding them. After all, the purpose of the education you are providing is that they take the necessary actions to get their own company up to speed so they can guarantee delivery of year 2000 compliant materials.

Whether you use a stick, when you introduce it, and how hard you apply it will all depend on your relationship with the supplier and how important it is to your operations. If suppliers are still unprepared to cooperate, have no illusions as to the risk placed on you. Even if you decide not to end the relationship, make sure that you have comprehensive contingency plans in case disaster strikes.

3. Customers

There are two issues that you need to remember when dealing with your customers. First, what competitive advantage can you extract from the fact that you may be the first one of their suppliers to bring this issue to their attention?

If you do it in the right way, you may well be able to show your customers that you are a company strategically thinking about important global issues. You may be able to impress their senior management by being the first in your industry or community to cover the *business* issues of the year 2000 problem. Or it may be that you can emphasize that of all their suppliers, you are the first — or soon will be — to be year 2000 compliant. While a customer may not be asking today if you are compliant, it may well be a standard question a year from now.

To sum up, if you can move your own plans along rapidly, you may gain a competitive edge with key existing customers, as well as potential new ones, by being able to show them how prepared you are for the next two years and into the next century.

Secondly, as you approach the millennium, the crucial issue will be a customer's credit worthiness. If one of your customers is not working on becoming Y2K compliant, or at the very least addressing the issue and its spin-offs, it is asking for financial trouble in the early part of the year 2000. And if it encounters those financial difficulties, one of the first things it will do is stop paying its suppliers — and that means you.

This is why it is so important that your sales and marketing personnel get under the skin of any new customer. You need to understand the customer's state of operations well beyond a Dun and Bradstreet report. If you do not do your homework, that dream contract of a million dollars could, in fact, spell the ruin of your business when your customer can't pay the bill.

PART IV

AND NOW FOR THE GOOD NEWS...

17
YEAR 2000 OPPORTUNITIES

There is some good news among all the doom and gloom, frightening costs, and predictions of human resource nightmares. In fact, there are some substantial opportunities for business. Companies that have recognized the problem early on and taken appropriate steps to deal with it may be in the best position to take advantage of these opportunities.

a. OPERATIONAL REVIEW

The year 2000 crisis will force you to take a comprehensive look at all of your corporate operations, and that is a good thing. Whether you realize it or not, all the steps you take to carry out your year 2000 plan — evaluating present systems, determining risk, identifying priorities, and deciding on solutions — are the same ones you would follow when conducting an operational review. While it is the year 2000 problem that is forcing you into this exercise, why not extract the maximum benefit from the process?

To evaluate your present systems, keep in the back of your mind any ideas you may have on how to improve them. Can you combine systems, streamline them, or simplify them? Are there opportunities to change job descriptions? Can you improve efficiency in certain operating areas with the addition of more computers or better training? Since you have to spend the money, or at least the time and effort to make sure that your systems will work into the next century, make sure that any resources you expend result in tangible business benefits.

Another advantage that comes from this operational review will be a complete and comprehensive look at all of your computer operations. For the first time, perhaps in the life of the company, you will have a complete and accurate list of all the hardware and software used in the business that you run. Are you using this equipment to its maximum efficiency? Are you encountering problems when staff members use different versions of the same software, such as having to convert spreadsheets or word-processing files back and forth? Many companies can continue to make effective use of older computers for internal use, such as word processing or e-mail. Are you making the most efficient use of your hardware?

The same evaluation should also be applied to all of your computer systems. While you may need to change your accounting system to make sure that it is year 2000 compliant, you may at the same time want to expand its operations to cover inventory control or order entry if these functions are not currently on-line. You may want to fill in awkward gaps between operations with appropriate bridging software, or with a brand new system altogether.

1. **ISO certification**

Your operational review might be done with an eye to becoming ISO certified, which can give you a competitive edge. An ISO-certified company is one that meets international standards for quality control. ISO (International Standards Organization) is the international authority that establishes world standards for manufacturing and processing.

There are different types of compliance. For example, ISO 9000 is a group of standards that in general relate to establishing different levels of quality control. Within this group, attaining ISO 9001 or 9002 certification means you are registered as internationally certified. A newer standard group is ISO 14000, which applies to environmental standards.

To meet these standards, you must carry out an analysis of your operations, develop written operating procedures for all of the steps involved in the production of your goods or services, and establish quality control procedures at every step.

ISO certification is vital for doing business abroad, particularly in Europe and Asia. It is also becoming more common in contracts arranged with U.S. firms.

It won't take much extra work to take the results of your operational review, document your procedures, and become ISO compliant. Having to deal with the year 2000 problem has its benefits, ones that hold a lot of potential for profit.

2. **Disaster recovery planning**

Now is the time to complete a comprehensive disaster recovery planned. Such a plan is, in effect, a series of steps that allow you to recover from any disaster — fire, flood, theft, or even an event such as the year 2000 problem!

Most companies never implement such a plan, usually because they think the odds of a disaster striking are too low to make it worthwhile. While floods and hurricanes are relatively rare, fire can strike at any time. And statistics show that in many cases an internal disaster — human error, equipment failure, or sabotage — happens far more frequently than most companies expect. Statistics show that most companies that undergo a flood or a fire cease operations if they cannot get up and running again within 30 days.

Your business's ability to recover quickly from a disaster will largely depend on your having up-to-date information about where the business was before the disaster happened. In other words, even if your insurance covers your building, computers, and other equipment, if you do not have accurate and up-to-date financial and operating information, your losses due to not having this data will probably be more than the company can bear.

Doing an operational review of your company to correct year 2000 procedures also provides you with the basic information you will need for effective disaster recovery planning. In fact, setting up such a plan is far easier than conforming to international standards and can often be helped through the purchase of some good software packages. An immediate benefit of such a plan can sometimes be lower insurance premiums.

In effect, your plan for the year 2000 is approximately 90% of the procedures you must undertake to complete your disaster recovery planning. With the addition of a complete schedule for backup of all company information, you may well find that this plan is now completely in place.

One possible advantage of going through the year 2000 process is that when you have completed it all, you may have built a company that is organized and controlled in the best possible way with the best possible systems. If you can accomplish this, you will be truly ready for the 21st century.

b. STRATEGIC PLANNING

An operational review generally looks at procedures that exist today and considers how they might be improved. These essentially are tactical decisions, i.e., decisions that will be carried out and that will affect company operations within the next one to two years at most. A related opportunity within this whole process stimulated by the year 2000 crisis is that you also can undergo a strategic planning process.

> Strategic planning takes the long view, from five to ten years ahead. Many companies argue that it is not possible to accurately predict that far into the future. That may be true, but strategic planning isn't about predicting minute details of corporate life ten years from now; it is about stepping back and looking at the big picture.

Strategic planning might include a closer look at operational trends within your industry. What is happening with human resources planning? Is there a shift to more part time, contract, or even shared jobs? Is there a movement out of major urban centers in order to reduce costs, or is the move in the opposite direction in order to be closer to major markets? What has happened to market share in the last ten years between domestic and foreign-owned companies? Will this trend continue, or were there special circumstances that will not be the same in the next ten years? What has happened with machinery and equipment that you use or that your suppliers use to produce your industry's product? What has been the overall trend of the use of computers in your industry? Has computer use grown? In what ways are computers used differently than they were ten years ago? What has been the biggest innovation in the last ten years? What has happened to industry concentration in the same time?

As Steven Covey says in his book *First Things First*, it does not matter whether you are moving at 1,000 miles per hour or 1,000,000 miles per hour; if you are moving in the wrong direction in the first place, speed is irrelevant. The questions above are just examples of a few of the strategic questions that you need to look at to help make sure that your company is moving in the right direction.

My usual recommendation to companies is that they have either a senior management or board of directors retreat to discuss some of the issues. In many ways, plans for January 1, 2000, consist of a typical strategic planning session, with some exceptional timetables and twists thrown in. A number of the decisions you make about your internal systems, as well your external partners such as customers and vendors, may well establish the style of your company for the next ten years. If that is the case, the interaction of all of its operations should be discussed by all of the managers of the various departments involved. It helps, too, to have input from a number of sage independent businesspeople who can look at the company more dispassionately than those involved in its day-to-day affairs.

Most owner-operators of small businesses reading this book will not have undertaken such an exercise ever in their business life. Again, I feel that the year 2000 problem has presented you with an opportunity that you would be foolish to pass up, particularly because the processes you will have to follow provide you with an immense amount of data on which you can make some of these important strategic decisions.

I have spent many years encouraging businesses to do strategic planning. While every company should have an up-to-date business plan, I understand all too well why it is difficult to do strategic long-term planning on an ongoing basis. The biggest challenge for many businesses is that they are so busy with their day-to-day operations, they have no time to spend looking at the horizon and figuring out how to get there.

The year 2000 forces everyone to look at that horizon and judge what the impact will be on business. What better time is there to use the information you collect to take a long hard look at how you can make things work better in the long run, regardless of any adjustments needed to pass January 1, 2000? I truly believe this is a significant opportunity in disguise.

c. YEAR 2000 CERTIFICATION

The advantage of becoming year 2000 certified earlier than other businesses may emerge as there becomes greater awareness of the problem. As companies of all sizes realize that the problem exists not only in their internal computer operations but also as a result of their relationships with their customers and suppliers, they will search out those partners that can demonstrate that all of their operations are year 2000 compliant.

Establishing this fact is, however, difficult at the present time. There are no standard international guidelines for year 2000 certification, so proving you are compliant and your customers and suppliers are compliant is a big challenge.

1. Proving your own compliance

It is difficult to prove that you are compliant. As you will find when you put together your year 2000 plan, it is a lengthy and changing process. Not only is it likely that the scope of your analysis will change, but additions and changes in staff, updates in technology and tools, and decisions to replace older systems will have a continuing impact on your operations. When a partner asks you 6 months into a 12-month process whether you are year 2000 compliant, what will be your honest reply?

2. **Proving your customers' and suppliers' compliance**

The certainty with which any company can claim to be year 2000 certified depends not only on its own plans and actions but also on those of its suppliers. Even if the company works diligently with all its existing partners, it must take certain statements on faith and trust that any actions being talked about are being undertaken.

In the previous chapter, I discussed the importance of having a comprehensive communications plan. I hope you will undertake this with all of your suppliers and customers. You may, however, find out that there are several hundred of these, ranging from mom-and-pop shops to companies with several hundred employees. It will not be possible for you to verify all of the information you receive. As well, if you determine that one or more of your suppliers is not ready for year 2000, you may have to spend a considerable amount of time finding a replacement that is. Until you are able to do so, you will be aware that part of your operations, while not presenting any problem on a day-to-day basis in 1998 and 1999, will not be year 2000 compliant. In theory, this will mean that your operation cannot be certified.

3. **International standards**

Currently, there are no universally agreed-upon international guidelines to establish formal year 2000 certification. For example, the American National Standards Institute (ANSI) has a *date field* standard, but it is not in harmony with the standard adopted by the International Standards Organization (ISO). The ANSI standard was adopted by the U.S. federal government for electronic data interchange (EDI) transactions. They now want to change it to a four-digit date field for the year. This only addresses the date-field standard, not year 2000 in its entirety.

The matching of ANSI, ISO, and other standards is a key issue. It could be used as a non-tariff trade barrier for North American products designed for export to the European

Union because of concerns about date-field interface problems. More significantly, all such inconsistencies will delay the production of a single globally accepted standard of year 2000 compliance.

Some industry groups aren't waiting. The Automotive Industry Action Group now promotes the use of a mandatory eight-digit date field (YYYYMMDD) for its members. It had to establish some uniform protocols so suppliers to the large automakers would receive computer data in a standard format, but it couldn't wait any longer for the standards bodies to catch up to the auto industry's needs. Other industries are also starting to move on their own because of this lack of generally accepted year 2000 principles.

There are obviously risks in certifying any organization that later proves to have systems that cannot work in the new century. The Information Technology Association of America (ITAA) has taken the approach that it will try and provide a year 2000 certificate to companies that can demonstrate that they have corrected their own systems as well as installing sufficient controls on the inputs and outputs of third parties. However, ITAA's sister organization, the Information Technology Association of Canada (ITAC), has decided that the liability attached in making such a guarantee is too much for it to carry. ITAC, therefore, has decided that it will not certify any company in Canada.

The logical organization that could assist in the standardization process is the federal government, but it is probably wishful thinking to believe that any bureaucratic organization can move swiftly enough to put such controls in place.

An approach that may help is to work with other members in your industry to ensure that as many companies as possible are up to speed on this issue. While on the one hand you may feel that you are assisting a competitor, this may be offset by the fact that you can share a lot of the workload. This may also help develop some innovative approaches that could assist all of you in your industry and/or community.

Despite all of this confusion, my advice to you is still to proceed to establish your company as year 2000 compliant. I am sure that in the coming months you will start to be asked more frequently whether you can meet these standards and whether you have the documentation to prove it. In the absence of any recognized international certification process, the best demonstration you can provide will be your overall year 2000 plans.

As awareness of the year 2000 problem increases, an increasing premium will be placed on the services of a company that is already year 2000 compliant. There have already been cases of contracts being won solely on the basis of a company's demonstrated commitment to ensuring that all of its systems and operations are in effect bug-free. You may find that you will be able to penetrate markets that were previously inaccessible, or you may find that this may be the unique selling point that allows you to beat out the competition for a premium contract.

You should start this process as soon as possible. Not only will this give you the maximum possible leverage in bidding situations such as those described above, but is it is also likely to keep your costs as low as possible.

d. TAKING ADVANTAGE OF MARKET CHANGES

You should expect that the year 2000 will bring significant changes in what companies service what markets in what geographic areas.

These changes will come as a result of any one of the factors already discussed. For example, a company may fail because it has not addressed the year 2000 issue. If there is a major disruption in transportation systems from its manufacturing facilities, it may be able to produce goods but be unable to deliver them. It may not be able to make financial arrangements because of problems at its bank. Any of these circumstances could mean that a market that might have been previously dominated by a foreign manufacturer may in fact be unserviced for several months or more. Depending on the nature of your business, this may offer an opportunity to penetrate a previously blocked market.

Another problem for some industries may be *too much* demand. We know today that we cannot fix all of the year 2000 problems by the turn of the century, even if everyone were fully aware and working on it immediately. Near the end of 1999 and into 2000 there will be a surge of panic buying for certain products as enterprises try to instantly fix their major year 2000 risks. A firm may usually produce 2,000 widgets a month, for example, but will now be asked to produce 20,000 year 2000–compliant widgets a month for the next year. It may well be forced to focus only on certain markets that it deems more strategic, which means withdrawing from other sales territories. Whether you are this firm or its competitor, market changes are bound to result.

Even within more local markets, there may be significant changes if one or more of your local competitors has operations that are hampered or even ended by the year 2000 problem. The Gartner Group, a think-tank in the United States, believes that over 30% of companies entering the new century will have done nothing to ensure that their systems work properly in the year 2000. You should continue to gather competitive intelligence on an ongoing basis about your competition, and perhaps adjust your marketing plans accordingly.

Note especially that a much higher percentage of foreign firms, including the Japanese and many European companies, will not be ready for the change in the millennium. One estimate suggests that over 70% of Far Eastern businesses will not be prepared for the year 2000. This will probably result in much more market churn than among better prepared North American competitors.

In a number of extreme cases, companies will fold because of the year 2000 problem. This may happen both before and after January 1, 2000. You may want to be on the lookout for such opportunities as they occur, or you may want to investigate the possibilities of a merger to strengthen your operations. You may be able to offer up-to-date systems and trained personnel to deal with the year 2000 situation; another company may be able to bring additional markets and/or production facilities not available to you at present. This is why working cooperatively on an industry-wide year 2000 committee may offer some distinct advantages. While you may sometimes be assisting your competitors, it is as likely that you will be boosting your industry as a whole, and in addition you may discover those potential partners interested in profitable mergers.

Even if companies in your industry do not merge, you may find that collectively you can tackle new markets that may be in considerable disarray following the start of the new millennium. This is something that only you can best judge: However my advice to you is to assume that it will *not* be business as usual on January 1, 2000.

e. THE YEAR 2000 INVESTOR

J.P. Morgan Securities, one of the largest banks and brokerage houses in the world, calls the year 2000 problem a $200 billion opportunity. At this stage, it is concentrating on two aspects of the problem. First, it too feels that it has to convince its clients and other investors that the problem is real. Second, it has a set of specific investment advice related to companies that directly or indirectly are involved with providing solutions — and parts of solutions — for the year 2000 conversion business.

As an investor, you may certainly want to follow this brokerage house's lead and investigate companies whose primary business will grow as a result of the year 2000 problem. Companies already involved in personnel placement will benefit as firms turn to them once they realize the need for new resources.

Another group includes companies such as SHL Systemhouse and other large consulting companies which provide a range of services, from acting as project managers to wholesale coordination of the whole exercise for larger organizations. There are software companies that are building tools that will assist in solving the problem, primarily by being able to examine older programming code intelligently, find the date fields and any resulting calculations, and fix them automatically. (Note that any fixes are not 100% certain and still require expert monitoring to make sure that they work properly.) Software companies that are in a position to provide year 2000 replacement software, such as Great Plains, will also benefit from increased sales and activities.

Another area of investment activity may rely more heavily on industry experts in each area. Within your own industry, for example, as you gather competitive information about your rivals and the changing state of the markets, you may be able to spot particular investment opportunities, given that you may have additional information and insights not available to the public at large.

As is always the case with investment advice, you should rely on quality expertise and information wherever you can find it. Although the Internet offers a full range of up-to-date facts and statistics, you must double check all the information you gather and use all of your data sources wisely. As financier Meyer Rothschild said more than 200 years ago, "the time to buy is when blood is flowing in the streets." There is no question in my mind that this year 2000 crisis will cause a lot of blood to flow, but from whose veins and in which streets is highly debatable.

One source of investment information is a book by Tony Keyes, *The Year 2000 Computer Crisis: An Investor's Survival Guide*. His philosophy is fairly conservative and he includes forecasts of some industry collapses. He also suggests some of the realities of wholesale changes that may well take place both before and after the start of the next millennium. You can visit his Web site at www.y2kinvestor.com.

PART V

AS THE WORLD TURNS

18
THE INTERNATIONAL SCENE

a. WHY IS SO LITTLE HAPPENING?

Much of the world is not ready for the year 2000 problem. Many of the world's governments are not moving forward on making sure that all of their systems are year 2000 compliant. There have been numerous stories about glitches caused by computer systems when dates in the new century are entered into their operations, such as the 104-year-old woman who was sent a notice asking her to attend kindergarten!

Governments in all parts of the world offer different excuses as to why they haven't started to tackle the issue. The first problem is that information technology managers may be reluctant to bring the issue forward. Government bureaucrats are even less prepared to admit mistakes or bad judgments than are private sector managers.

Governments also have a few reasons of their own:

(a) *No money.* Many world economies are not in good shape, and those that are have far more demands placed on available funds than they can support. Since solving the year 2000 problem brings few if any benefits that can be trumpeted to the electorate as government accomplishments, spending heavily on solving it is not high on a bureaucratic list of priorities.

(b) *Short time frame.* Some government departments have been working on correcting their systems for the year 2000 bug for more than a decade. Unfortunately, this is the exception rather than the rule. Democratic institutions by their very nature tend to deal in short time frames, e.g., the four years to the next election. They can't afford to spend time planning for the distant future. This may have meant that in the early part of the 1990s the results of the year 2000 problem were too far away to worry about. Whatever the justification, there was little if any action taken by most governments in the early part of this decade.

(c) *Level of computerization.* Living in North America, we tend to assume that every government and every business relies on computers as much as we do. This is not the case in most of the developing world. Governments and most larger companies will be using computers, but the vast majority of economic structures will have very little in the way of electronic equipment.

There are also some cultural differences that have prolonged the inaction.

1. **Difference in calendars**

Some cultures using different calendars assume that the year 2000 won't affect them. For example, under the Jewish calendar, the year 1997 is 5758; under the Islamic calendar it is 1418. The Chinese year is different again. But what governments in those countries don't understand is that their computer systems came from the West and are in fact following the Western Julian calendar.

When a computer system in Saudi Arabia, for example, receives a request that involves a date calculation based on the Islamic calendar, it goes through a number of steps. First, it translates the date from the Islamic form to the Julian (Western-style) calendar. Then when it has done the required calculations and has the result in Julian form, it reconverts it back to the Islamic calendar. All of this happens unknown to the user, of course, so the average person assumes that the computer and all of its related chips and programs are immune to the year 2000 bug.

2. **Concept of time**

Even in industrialized countries where there is great focus on precise time measurements and the keeping of timetables, it is hard to get the message across that the year 2000 problem has an absolute and irrevocable drop-dead date. Cultures that aren't part of the industrial world have a different concept of time, and it is that much more difficult to get people fired up to the point where lengthy delays must be regarded as critical.

3. **Government processes**

Even when the issue is understood and government leaders urgently call for immediate action and rapid response, further delays result because of the government's own purchasing procedures.

Over the last two or three decades, many governments have joined together in trading alliances, such as the European

Union, NAFTA, and ASEAN. As part of their agreements within such bodies, governments have passed legislation and guidelines to ensure that bidding on government contracts is open and above board in order to allow companies from the other countries covered by the agreement to bid on another government's work. Part of the process to allow a level playing field is that there are often absolute built-in time frames. Often, the bigger the contract, the more rigorous are the fairness rules. In Canada and the United States, for example, the bidding process on a request for proposal (RFP) for a major project is typically nine months long.

Such RFPs are typically issued individually by each department or ministry. Since some of these bureaucrats are only just becoming aware today that they have a millennium problem, the challenge they now face is that there may be a nine-month delay built in before they can even hire the proper resources to start corrective action.

This situation becomes further entangled when lawyers get involved. I have seen RFPs that include the requirement to deposit huge performance bonds and absolute legal guarantees that the project will be 100% certain, complete, and without problem by December 31, 1999. And the penalties included in these contracts are often ruinous. What government bureaucrats and their legal advisers have not realized about the year 2000 situation is that there is far more work available for the various consultants and experts than they can handle. This means that they can turn down whatever work is not sufficiently rewarding or which carries undue risk. The sorts of government contracts that are being proposed are often cheap and risky, and in some cases this has meant that no bids are tendered.

The U.S. Internal Revenue Service recently submitted an RFP for the year 2000 conversion of many of its systems. Over 150 pages of the contract dealt with the items mentioned above, that is, performance bonds, guarantees, and penalties. The department apparently received only two responses. One was from a major computer manufacturer, which submitted a proposal subject to the complete renegotiation of all of these last 150 pages. The other was from a large systems integrator. This organization supposedly offered to do all of the work involved for $1, provided that in return, it receive the right to operate all IRS systems, as well as the right to charge fees to all IRS customers, for the next 50 years. I understand this latter proposal was turned down on the basis of national security concerns.

There is an enormous gulf in understanding between those asking for year 2000 services and those who are able to provide them. Usually the purchaser is in the driver's seat because he or she has the ability to demand a fixed price or select who gets the contract. In the case of the millennium bug, however, all the rules change. It is the contractor who is far more able to determine the terms of the deal.

b. AROUND THE GLOBE

At the time of writing in August 1997, it appears that less than a quarter of the world's countries have started on the year 2000 problem. An alarming number of governments fail to recognize that there is any problem at all.

Though there seems to be a high degree of awareness in English-speaking industrialized countries — where the majority of computer programmers reside — the degree of preparedness varies widely. There is also a considerable difference between private sector readiness and public sector readiness in each nation.

Different countries' readiness is hard to evaluate objectively. As might be expected, all official government announcements continue to insist that everything will be completely ready by the turn of the century. On the other hand, there are always government bureaucrats (who will speak off the record only) who will tell you that this is not the case and may provide chapter and verse as to which systems in which departments are certain to collapse when the new millennium begins.

So while I am encouraged by most of the news that I hear about progress in North America, I am not blindly optimistic that every department in either the Canadian or the U.S. federal government will work perfectly. Nor can I be certain that the most critical ones are those that are guaranteed to work. Unfortunately, I am very pessimistic about a large number of governments.

In my evaluation below of what different countries and regions are doing about the year 2000 problem, I examine three things: awareness within the country, government action at different levels, and private sector activities.

In almost all countries, whether you talk about the public or private sectors, there is a direct correlation between the size of the operation and its activities. In other words, big business and big government are usually aware of the problem and doing something about it, medium-sized government and businesses are only semi-aware and half-prepared, and small organizations are almost completely oblivious to the problem.

Note that the comments are general and focus only on those countries from which there is news about year 2000 readiness.

1. Canada

The Gartner Group's recent survey of year 2000 preparedness of countries around the globe confirms that Canada is ahead of the rest of the world — with the possible exception of Australia. It must be admitted that in the initial stages, much of this preparedness was more a matter of luck than good planning, but whatever the reason, a lot of its major systems are going to be ready for the date change on December 31, 1999.

There are a couple of factors that added to Canada's preparedness for the millennium bug. One is the presence of Peter de Jager, one of the earliest and now certainly one of the best-known prophets about the year 2000 problem. De Jager first came to prominence in an article he wrote for *Computer World Magazine* on September 6, 1993, entitled "Doomsday," which is often recognized as one of the earliest call to arms on this problem. He has been consciousness-raising for over four years — which is four years longer than many other year 2000 experts now on the scene.

Canada's other advantage is the number of its key industries controlled by monopolies: the banking, power, and telecommunications industries. Because they are such large companies, they became aware of the problem early on. Over the last five or more years, they will have steadily devoted sufficient time and resources to address and solve the problem.

Below the level of these large conglomerates, however, much of Canada's industrial infrastructure remains at considerable risk. Canada has a large number of technology industries and human resources but will still face the same problem as the rest of the world in that these resources will fall far short of the eventual need. Many of the large consulting firms are already working at capacity and not taking on new clients. And Ontario, the industrial heartland of Canada, may be the one province where awareness of the problem is the lowest.

In the public sector, Canada's preparedness varies tremendously. In many cases, year 2000 coordinators have been appointed, but whether they all have the appropriate authority, responsibility, budget, or resources is very uncertain. The federal government's critical systems appear to be in reasonable shape. It is a great deal less certain that the provincial governments are equally prepared.

Several federal government departments have been working on the issue for more than ten years, and all of them now have active plans. In general, Y2K is receiving an increasing amount of attention, and most major systems should be well in hand by January 1, 1999, leaving all of that year available for testing and fine-tuning.

Activities of all government departments are overseen by the Treasury Board Secretariat and the Chief Information Officer, Paul Rummell. There is a coordinating committee made up of top senior bureaucrats from all ministries and departments. The year 2000 is a regular agenda item on the monthly meetings of all deputy ministers. And despite recent criticisms from Canada's Auditor General, the federal government has streamlined the RFP process related to year 2000 and is about to tender over $100 million of related work before the end of 1997. A lot of progress is being made, and while not all systems will be ready in time, I believe that it is unlikely that there will be any major disasters at the federal level.

At the provincial level, less progress has been made. From some reports, it appears that a preliminary sizing of the problem has been completed, and structured, detailed estimates are in process. Many systems are in the process of being upgraded. The lack of information in itself suggests a problem. If there were a lot of progress being made, it would be being loudly announced, assuming provincial governments understand the significance of such progress in the first place.

Apart from initial analysis and planning, few public sector organizations at the provincial level have started to repair or replace vulnerable systems. Almost unanimously, interviewees perceive that there is a lack of appreciation for the seriousness of the problem at the most senior levels of government. The cost estimates that should be provided are very large, typically 15% to 25% of the government's annual information technology (IT) expenditures. These costs are not reflected in most IT plans, and instructions continue to be issued that any dollars spent must be made from within existing budgets.

An additional problem is that two of the largest provinces, Ontario and Alberta, are under the control of extremely conservative governments and have been for the last several years. Both of these provinces have been going through radical downsizing and cost-cutting exercises. Given this environment, it is highly unlikely that any IT departments within specific ministries have been given appropriate budgets to deal with the year 2000 problem.

Ontario has one other particular problem. The provincial government has just forced through an enormous number of changes altering who is responsible for which programs between provincial and municipal authorities. Responsibility for welfare administration is one of the items that has been downloaded to the local governments of municipalities and townships. This transfer will be accomplished just in time for the new millennium, putting an acute social responsibility into systems right at the time that the computers trying to administer them may be shutting down entirely.

The state of the municipalities is even worse, although this does depend on the size of the city or town involved. Ottawa Carleton is well advanced in its preparations — as you might expect for a municipality that houses the federal government and is the center of Canada's Silicon Valley North. Toronto, however, is far less aware and consequently less prepared.

Most of the smaller municipalities and townships are completely oblivious to the problem and have absolutely no plans in place to deal with it — before or after.

In summary, the current estimate, based on reliable sources, is that the cost to the provinces and the federal government will be on the order of $1 billion over the next three years. Most jurisdictions expect these estimates to grow substantially. Cost estimates are likely to increase as the scope of analysis is extended to include desktop software and hardware. In addition, the cost of year 2000 projects borne by public sector agencies, boards, commissions, and crown corporations are not included in most government estimates.

2. United States

Until recently, there was an extremely low level of awareness of the year 2000 problem in the United States. This may have resulted from a lack of leadership at the highest levels of government, fewer monopolies compared to Canada, or some other cause. However, this has changed and the U.S. may be now outstripping other countries in its efforts to make it a public issue. However, it still faces the formidable hurdles of limited resources and lack of time.

It is perhaps ironic that one of the groups doing the most to raise awareness is the legal profession. If $600 billion seems an unimaginable figure to you — the cost of converting all systems — imagine adding on *five times that amount* for legal bills. The United States is already seen as being one of the most litigious countries in the world, and it appears that it is going to get worse. One cannot conceive of that amount of money flowing through the legal system without it having a negative effect on truly productive elements of the economy.

The U.S. Office of Management and Budget (OMB) issued a report on February 6, 1997, entitled "Getting Federal Computers Ready for 2000." The report's conclusion is that the federal government is making considerable progress in addressing the year 2000 problem in federal computer systems. The office admits there is a lot of work to be done and a limited time frame, but concludes that the "problem will be solved without disruption of federal programs."

However, looking at some of the details of the report can leave you more doubtful. Two items stand out in particular. First, the budget that the OMB said would be needed was approximately $2.3 billion. Since the Canadian government, which is one-tenth the size, is now expecting to spend more than $1 billion (and that figure is constantly rising), the U.S. estimate appears to be dangerously low. Certainly it is well below what other industry and year 2000 experts suggest is the more accurate figure, which they place at between $20 and $30 billion. Such a low estimate suggests either a level of naiveté in the amount calculations or of an ongoing bureaucratic attitude that it is still necessary to downplay the size of the problem. Either of these attitudes is cause for great concern about the government's understanding of the issue.

The other item that stands out is the government's proposed schedule for completion. Of the 27 departments listed, 9 of them will become compliant only in December 1999. An additional 15 will only do so in October and November of 1999. This means that a total of 24 out of 27 departments, or almost 89% of them, will be ready only three months or less before the start of the 21st century.

The person in charge of the entire federal effort is Sally Katzen, Administrator of the Office of Regulatory Affairs of the OMB. Katzen made it clear that it is not her role to get the job done. That responsibility lies with the separate agencies and the military. Her role is defined as "resolving conflicts and assuring coordination" among the agencies. They will each remain responsible for setting their own timetables and for gathering the necessary resources to complete the conversion. She continues to issue statements reassuring the public that everything will be completed on time.

I suggest that the probability of the OMB schedule being met is extremely low. This skepticism is shared by several of the representatives of the U.S. Congress and Senate. This past summer, the House Science Subcommittee under the direction of Congressman Steven Horn (R-CA) issued an appeal to the president to take a leadership role in the year 2000 conflict. Congresswoman Connie Morella (R-MD) has issued a similar plea, as has Senator Daniel Patrick Moynihan (D-NY). Note that when it comes to the year 2000 problem, concern runs across party lines. To date President Clinton has not taken any such role.

On September 15, 1997, Congressman Steven Horn issued his second annual grades for year 2000 preparedness. Of the 24 agencies reviewed, 11 received a D or lower. Departments that received this failing grade included Commerce, Energy, Justice, Nuclear Regulation, Agriculture, Treasury, Education, and Transportation. And the trends for most of these were down from his first set of evaluations a year earlier. This grade report says it all.

At the state level, there is a wide range of readiness, but activities appear to be accelerating quickly. Some states have also undertaken innovative schemes for financing and accelerating the project. For example, Nebraska has added a 2¢ tax to each package of cigarettes, the money going directly to year 2000 remediation efforts. In New York, the governor has recently banned all non-essential IT projects if they will impact an agency's ability to achieve date compliance. Similar measures have been proposed in California.

There is very little that can be reported for activities at the lower levels of the U.S. government infrastructure. Unfortunately, the only valid interpretation that can be placed on this lack of news is a complete lack of awareness, plans, or progress.

Outside of government, I fear that the biggest problems may be with the U.S. banking system. If the financial organizations don't work, then everything else shuts down, either directly or indirectly as a result of the domino effect. There are 6,000 banks in the United States, all heavily linked together. If a significant number of them are unable to operate, the impact could be catastrophic.

In a recent report from Reuters, senior representatives from the Securities and Exchange Commission (SEC) and Federal Deposit Insurance Corporation (FDIC) assured the Senate Banking Committee that they were well aware of the size and seriousness of the problem. The regulators say their concern is with smaller institutions. Some 10% of smaller banks are more or less unaware of the millennium problem and its potential impact on their businesses.

First, bank customers will be affected. Even though a company might have sufficient funds in its bank account, the bank may be unable to verify this. So the private enterprise will not be able to make payments by check or meet its payroll, which means that private enterprise is at risk. Second, any bank linked to the one with failed systems will also start to be unable to complete transactions, which then starts to have a domino effect on its own operations.

3. Europe

The European Union (E.U.) has some unique considerations regarding year 2000. The use of the new Euro-dollar has huge implications and complications. Record keeping of sales between two companies in different countries becomes markedly more complicated. The tracking of gains or losses due to foreign currency fluctuations will become doubly complicated. Even the concept of decimal points is a problem for some countries (e.g., Italy), which have not had to deal with them for at least the last 50 years.

The biggest problem that the Euro-dollar brings is that up until now, all the IT professionals in Europe have concentrated solely on that issue and have had no time to examine the impact of the year 2000 on their company's operations.

Whether one examines the public or private sector in any European country, the activity is preliminary at best, and in some cases almost entirely lacking.

England may have the highest state of awareness in the world due in large part to a large and very visible public awareness campaign conducted by a two-person coordinating committee. Unfortunately, this has not had the success it should have had in terms of companies taking up the challenge, although activity there is accelerating too.

If new computer systems have to be installed to deal with the new European standards, both financial and nonfinancial, these replacements may deal with the year 2000 concerns automatically. But given the complete lack of substantive news coming out of the E.U., this is probably the most optimistic view of the situation.

4. Russia and Eastern Europe

Although the state of computers in the former Eastern Bloc has always lagged far behind that of the West, this may place Russia and Eastern Europe almost more at risk than operations in, for example, North America. Why? Because in lacking PCs, far more of their systems are based on mainframes, and far more of their systems represent decades of layers of archaic code with no upgrades or changes from their original foundations.

Mikhail Gorbachev was supposed to appear recently at a press conference in California to emphasize the size of the risk that year 2000 represented to ongoing computer operations in Russia. The meeting did not take place, but the problem he was going to talk about has not gone away, and is substantial. Any comments made regarding Russia will also apply to other countries of the former Soviet Union. Countries that have adopted large numbers of personal computers in the last few years are also at risk because, of course, those PCs are also not year 2000 compliant.

5. Asia

The news from Asia is patchy. This in itself is worrisome, given that if a series of activities are not happening on a number of fronts, a country's operations may be at considerable risk because of the domino effect.

Much of the commentary available on action in Asia relates to the financial community. In Singapore, a recent report stated that 40% of its banks still have no plans for year 2000 conversion. Hong Kong banks have increased their activities since the mid-1996 report card. However, 5% still have no activity under way, and another 14% have not yet finalized their plans. If these statistics are accurate, it almost guarantees that within hours of the new millennium, these banks' erroneous data or inability to complete transactions will corrupt the operations of the rest of the banks in that community.

In London, England, one of the centers of global finance, the financial community has apparently already started to consider contingency measures based on the expectation that there will be parts of the world's financial economy that it will have to isolate. In other words, if it discovers that the data from a financial center such as Singapore is untrustworthy, it wants established procedures by which it can, in effect, eliminate Singapore from the global network. Given the integrated nature of the world's economies, that London is even considering such measures is scary indeed.

One country that is, perhaps surprisingly, not doing a lot about the problem is Japan. It has a low degree of awareness despite there being more large enterprises with mainframe legacy applications in Japan than in almost any other country. The problem is also more severe because 70% of software applications in Japan are customized, as opposed to 75% in the United States being packaged.

Although there is little news coming out of China, there is reason to believe that some action may be starting. On

October 8, 1997, the Beijing State Science and Technology Commission, working with the Ministry of Electronics, announced that China has slapped an import ban on all computers with two-digit time counting systems.

Lack of progress around the world was emphasized at the recent Semiconductor '97 Forum in an address by Manny Hernandez of Dataquest. He said, "By December 31, 1999, 80% of U.S. companies and 65% of European companies will be in compliance. In contrast, only 27% of the rest of the world, including Japan, will be ready."

6. South Pacific

The Gartner Group's most recent survey suggests that of all the countries of the world, Australia is the farthest ahead in preparations for the millennium date change. From the information available on the Internet and public announcements, both the federal and state governments seem to have plans in place. There also seems to be much awareness in the private sector.

New Zealand is moving much more slowly than Australia, but it too seems to have an increasing awareness of the problems it will face. The Leader of the Opposition in the New Zealand parliament, Peter Dunne, is taking the initiative in raising the overall awareness of the Y2K problem. He is aggressively raising the issue within the government, including proposing a bill that would require every company in the country to conduct a year 2000 audit.

Apart from these two countries, there seems to be little activity in the South Pacific community. In fact, most year 2000 discussions are on the problem of how to accommodate possibly thousands of tourists who wish to be on the dateline so that they can be the first in the world to greet the new millennium. Both tourists and the countries involved may be in for a nasty shock!

19
CONCLUSION

This book has been designed to give you the tools with which to move into the 21st century with anticipation and confidence in the future, rather than spending your time burdened with the mistakes of the past. I hope that it has helped you in this respect. But if we are going to come out of this crisis with the minimum possible pain and, frankly, the greatest possible international gain, we must start to sound every possible alarm bell at every possible level to make sure that we are not casualties of the process.

We can all do something to help solve this problem. What we can do about the year 2000 crisis depends in part on ourselves as individuals and the positions we hold at work. Some of us may have enough to do as employees and voters. Others who belong to volunteer, community, business, or political associations may be able to take on a bigger role.

The major problem at the moment is the lack of awareness of the crisis. Armed with the information I have provided, every one of us, no matter what our part in the community, can go out and start instilling that knowledge in other people.

This chapter summarizes how you might best do that, depending on which hat you wear.

a. OWNERS, MANAGERS, AND SENIOR EXECUTIVES

Clearly, the place to start is in your own backyard. Depending on your position within the company, you may be able to immediately initiate the appropriate awareness and planning processes, or you may have to start educating your fellow executives.

Following the process laid out in chapter 10 should certainly help you formulate the best plans for your enterprise. As you go through the various steps, keep in mind that as you educate your staff, suppliers, customers, and other contacts, you are also helping raise the awareness of the general public. Each seed you plant will spur the awareness and activity that we all need if we are going to meet and surmount this challenge.

b. EMPLOYEES

While it may be more difficult for you to have an immediate impact, and more time consuming too, you should also start to educate any and all of your coworkers. Talking to your boss is a good start. If you can, make sure that any discussion includes the financial risk to the company if it fails to take the appropriate steps. This is a method that is likely to get the attention of supervisors and senior managers.

If you are chosen to coordinate your company's year 2000 activities, make sure you have the necessary support and resources. This could be a career-enhancing move, provided your boss does not have unrealistic expectations. If you are not given appropriate authority to get the job done, it could be a disaster for both the company and you.

c. PROFESSIONALS AND CONSULTANTS

As companies become more aware of the year 2000 problem, they will recognize that they need more expert resources. No matter what your professional expertise, you will be well served to learn as much as you can about the impact of the millennium bug in your particular line of work.

In the accounting and legal professions, there will certainly be opportunities to spend all of your time developing and then working on this particular specialty. In other professions, too, an understanding of the year 2000 problem will put you ahead of your competitors and help you stand out from the crowd.

d. ASSOCIATION MEMBERS

Whatever association you may belong to, here is the place where you can have the most immediate impact. It does not matter whether the association is related to a particular business or community, whether it is technical or non-technical, or whether it appears to have any connection with the year 2000 problem. As you now understand, all associations are affected.

> Don't ignore organizations outside the business world. Churches, day care centers, and even parent-teacher associations offer opportunities for you to talk about the problem with other people. If you feel a little awkward raising the issue now, think about how visionary you will appear in three or six months' time when everyone will be talking about the problem.

---

e. CONSUMERS

Much of this book has been written to aid the businessperson in understanding what this challenge will mean to his or her company. Its impact is so pervasive that even your role as consumer will be affected.

As you buy anything, you should be talking about the year 2000 issue. Obviously purchases such as alarm systems, electronic equipment, computers, and other items will be directly affected by computer date chip compliance and you should discuss the issue with every potential vendor. Start asking year 2000 questions at your favorite dress shop or corner delicatessen. They, too, need to understand as soon as possible that their business is at risk. If you don't tell them, who will? And if you don't tell them now, the three- or six-month wait until they understand the issues might be the crucial period when they should have been making their preparations.

f. VOTERS

If there is a single area where we can all have an impact, it is as an informed voter asking questions of our elected officials. Even if many people think of the year 2000 problem as pertaining only to big computer systems — and we know that this is not the case — this means that government systems are severely at risk.

In earlier chapters I outlined what various levels of government are doing — and not doing. It should be clear from this discussion that there is bound to be at least one set of elected officials who both need more information and who also need to get some additional pressure placed on them to start initiating immediate action. In some cases this will be the federal government. In other cases you will need to raise your concerns at the state or provincial level. In almost every case, your local government will be woefully unprepared.

No matter what level of government or department you are addressing, take up the issue right away. Don't let government get away with pat reassurances that everything is under control. Challenge government with the issue on election day. Ask about it at public debate. Inform your local media about the problem and have it ask the questions at the appropriate time.

If this is indeed a challenge for all of us, all of our institutions and all of our communities, then we must all become involved. Even though this is a global issue and something that must be addressed at the highest levels, there is much we can do at the grassroots level as well. As voters we can make our voices heard and put some muscle behind our words and concerns.

g. MORE SUPPORT FROM US

HighSpin Corporation was founded to translate the confusing and jargon-filled commentary about the latest technology into practical business advice for the owners and executives of small- and medium-sized enterprises. Over the years we have developed programs to supply information about the latest developments in computers, telecommunications, satellites, cell phones, the Internet, alternative power sources, business processes, and transportation methods and how they apply in a *practical* way to the average business.

But when we started looking at the year 2000 problem, we realized that this was something that required our full concentration. Here was a topic that had to be communicated to all businesses at the greatest possible speed and in the loudest and clearest possible voice. We are now dedicated to informing everyone we can reach about the year 2000 problem and what can be done about it.

Besides this book, we are developing a series of other products to help companies understand the challenge and then teach them the best way to deal with it. Much of our time is spent giving seminars in centers across North America, to both public and private audiences.

We always welcome comment and feedback about the information we provide, and would be happy to give you more information about our services. We can be reached at our offices in Ottawa at (613) 692-0752, or by fax at (613) 692-5033. Our Web site is at www.highspin.com, and comments via e-mail can be sent to feedback@highspin.com.

I look forward to hearing from you. I truly hope that January 1, 2000, is the start of a happy New Year!

APPENDIX 1
A checklist for chief executive officers of small- and medium-sized enterprises

"Many senior executives are going to find it a shocking revelation when they finally realize the risks to which their organizations are exposed."
— Peter Broadmore, vice president,
Information Technology Association of Canada (ITAC).

☐ Have you a year 2000 champion at board level? (Year 2000 programs have a significant impact on business strategy and resources. Risk of failure is high without a senior champion to fight for funds, staff, and attention.)

☐ Have you communicated to your staff the goals of your year 2000 program and your commitment to realize them? (It is vital that business unit managers, with year 2000–affected business systems, understand that date processing problems may cause the failure of their business process, and that they take responsibility for the solution.)

☐ Have you appointed a year 2000 program manager, with sufficient authority to make difficult business decisions on behalf of your company?

☐ Have you provided your year 2000 program manager with an open door to the most senior decision makers in the company, to address situations where higher authority is required?

- [ ] Have your contracting, purchasing, and internal system development policies been modified to block the acquisition or development of additional year 2000 non-compliant systems?

- [ ] Have you completed an inventory of year 2000 date-sensitive information technology and facilities assets? (The inventory should include manufacturing and business systems, computer hardware, date-sensitive communications, and facilities systems, e.g., PBXs, building access, fire systems, elevators, power supply, air-conditioning.)

- [ ] Have your company's critical systems been identified? (Involve business unit managers early to identify business-critical systems.)

- [ ] Has responsibility for the year 2000 compliance of each system been clearly assigned? (E.g., business unit manager, in-house team, outsourcing organization, software product supplier.)

- [ ] Is the assessment and triage of your information technology holdings complete? (Time is becoming critically short. Many companies spend too much time in the assessment and planning phase of their program: 20% is reasonable.)

- [ ] Have you approved and adequately funded a year 2000 conversion program? (Once into the conversion process, many companies encounter unexpected problems that can increase effort and cost to as much as four times the original estimate. While needs vary by company, plans resourced at less than one-third of normal IT budgets in each of the next four years are likely to be inadequate. Where resources have been diverted from other business activities, hostility to the year 2000 program can be expected and must be managed by senior executives.)

☐ Is your year 2000 conversion plan synchronized with your business partners'? (Have all EDI (electronic data interchange) or data links with customers, suppliers, and key business partners been fully addressed?)

☐ Is year 2000 conversion underway? (It is important to begin conversion of several systems quickly. Year 2000 conversions pose unfamiliar business and technical challenges. Successful companies report significant "learning by doing.")

☐ Are you ready to deal with the threatened or real loss of your key year 2000 managers and IT professionals? (Local and international competition for year 2000 practitioners is cut-throat. Corporate compensation policies and practices must be reviewed now to create the flexibility needed to retain and replace key year 2000 professionals.)

☐ Does your test plan provide adequate resources, time, and contractual access to off-site test facilities? (Few companies plan sufficient time and effort for this vital phase of their year 2000 program; testing may require 50% or more of program time and resources. And few companies have sufficient in-house IT capacity or technical expertise to complete this vital phase of their year 2000 program without assistance.

APPENDIX 2
Resources

a. BOOKS

The last time I checked, there were about 25 books on the year 2000 problem in print. The ones listed below are those that may be most relevant to the individual, owner of a small- or medium-sized business, or consumer. I have not read all these books, so please check to see whether they are appropriate to your needs. Also, as January 1, 2000, draws nearer, the advice contained within these books may become less relevant depending on the time frames they suggest is required.

Finding and Fixing Your Year 2000 Problem: A Hands-On Guide for Small Organizations and Workgroups, by Jesse Feiler and Barbara Butler (Ap Professional, 1997)

Managing '00: Surviving the Year 2000 Computing Crisis, by Peter de Jager and Richard Bergeon (John Wiley & Sons, 1997)

A Survival Guide for the Year 2000 Problem, by Jim Lord (self-published, 1997)

Time Bomb 2000: What the Year 2000 Computer Crisis Means to You!, by Edward and Jennifer Yourdon (Prentice Hall, 1998)

The Year 2000 Computer Crisis, An Investor's Survival Guide, by Tony Keyes (Y2K Investor, 1997)

Year 2000 Solutions: A Manager's Guide to the Impending Collapse of Every IT System, by Stewart S. Miller (Springer Verlag, 1997)

Year 2000 Solutions for Dummies, by K.C. Bourne (IDG Books Worldwide, 1997)

b. WEB SITES

The Internet is really the best place to get up-to-date information about the year 2000 problem, although there is so much information out there it is sometimes difficult to narrow in on what you want. Below are my own top 13 sites, with a brief description of each.

    As well, I would recommend the newsgroup comp.software.year-2000. Much of the commentary on this newsgroup is from people who have been in the programming profession for 20 or 30 years. They are very helpful if you have a particular question, but don't approach them from a know-it-all position or they'll slice you to ribbons!

    Although these addresses were current at the time of writing, material on the Internet changes quickly, and it is possible that some of these addresses may be defunct or have changed when you try to access them.

2k-Times
Some excellent writing is often buried within the list of articles, but probably the best set of links that I have come across on the Web.
www.2k-times.com/y2klinks.htm

The Computer Information Centre - Year 2000 Date Problem - Support Centre
One of the best-organized sites, well documented, with particularly good European (which at present tends to mean U.K.) information.
www.compinfo.co.uk/y2k.htm

Ed Yourdon and Jennifer Yourdon's Time Bomb 2000
The best site I know for the impact of the year 2000 on the consumer. Alternatively, buy their book!
www.yourdon.com

Electric Utilities and Y2K
The name describes it! Tends to focus on U.S. utilities, but a must for people and businesses concerned about how utilities are doing (or not doing).
www.accsyst.com/writers/ele2000a.htm

Gary North's Y2K Links and Forums
Opinionated and very right-wing in viewpoint, but one of the first Y2K sites, with an enormous number of articles under a variety of topics archived over the last two years.
www.garynorth.com

Information Technology Association of America (ITAA)
General association site, but with a reasonable Y2K section. Subscribe to its e-mail newsletter to get up-to-date news from around the world.
www.itaa.org

Information Technology Exchange -Year/2000 Journal
The Year2000 Information Network claims to be North America's fastest-growing network of IT professionals specializing in managing the year 2000 problem.
www.mbs-program.com

JBA Year 2000 Web Site
Private sector year 2000 solutions provider, but still with a lot of articles and other information. Good description of basic problem.
www.jbaintl.com

Westergaard Year 2000
This site is the official gadfly to the U.S. government and private sector. Thank heavens someone is! Short readable articles, commentary, and analysis constantly updated.
www.y2ktimebomb.com

www.Y2K com, Legal and Management Information
Site in association with a law firm in Washington, D.C., but good discussions of legal issues and excellent links page.
www.y2k.com

Y2K Investor
Good site for the investment and broader economic implications of year 2000, both from an institutional and individual point of view.
www.y2kinvestor.com

Year 2000 Information Center
Probably the best-known site in the world, from Peter de Jager, the man who first raised the Y2K alarm. Lots of information but indifferently organized. Good e-mail newsletter, but a little too self-promotional. Note that the list of Y2K solution providers is paid advertising.
www.year2000.com

Year 2000 Webring
Year 2000 Webring is a collection of Year 2000 sites linked together to form a ring, meaning you can go from one to the next in a circle. If you find a site that is part of this group, you will then be able to go through 50 or more sites all related to the Y2K problem. Many of them are for solution providers of some kind, but it is still a useful way of finding sites that may not be linked elsewhere.